Thomas Francis Knox

When does the Church Speak Infallibly?

Or the Nature and Scope of the Church's Teaching Office. Second Edition

Thomas Francis Knox

When does the Church Speak Infallibly?
Or the Nature and Scope of the Church's Teaching Office. Second Edition

ISBN/EAN: 9783337030360

Printed in Europe, USA, Canada, Australia, Japan

Cover: Foto ©Lupo / pixelio.de

More available books at **www.hansebooks.com**

WHEN DOES THE CHURCH SPEAK INFALLIBLY?

WHEN DOES THE CHURCH SPEAK INFALLIBLY?

OR,

THE NATURE AND SCOPE OF THE CHURCH'S TEACHING OFFICE.

BY

THOMAS FRANCIS KNOX,

OF THE LONDON ORATORY.

"The Church of the living God, the pillar and ground of the truth." 1 Tim. iii. 15.

SECOND EDITION, ENLARGED.

LONDON:
BURNS, OATES, & CO.
17 PORTMAN STREET, AND 63 PATERNOSTER ROW.
MDCCCLXX.

WYMAN AND SONS,
GREAT QUEEN STREET, LINCOLN'S INN FIELDS,
LONDON, W.C.

PREFACE.

The following pages are addressed to Catholics who, as such, necessarily believe that Christ has provided us in the Church with an infallible teacher. The fact, therefore, of the Church's infallibility as teacher is assumed as the starting-point. But, taking this for granted, various questions, speculative and practical, of the deepest importance naturally suggest themselves, and they must be answered if the Church's teaching office is to become an actual and living reality. Thus, if her teaching is to be of any practical avail to us, we must know what are the organs by which she teaches infallibly, what are the subjects about which her teaching is infallible, what is the mode of her teaching, and what the obligation in conscience that it lays upon us. These are questions which press for an answer. And upon the answer given to them the whole tone of a man's bearing towards the Church and secular science will depend. It seemed, therefore, that a short and connected statement of the Church's teaching on these points would not be useless, especially at the present time, when attention has been more or less directed to this subject. It was under this impression that the following tract was written. It has no pretensions to be a theological and scientific treatise. But the sole object aimed at has been to present to ordinary readers a brief and simple account of the nature of the Church's office as our infallible teacher, according to her own view of it, and the received doctrine of approved theologians.

THE ORATORY, LONDON,
 Trinity Sunday, 1867.

PREFACE TO SECOND EDITION.

THE first edition of this little work was published in the form of a pamphlet. The favourable reception which it has met with, both at home and on the Continent, especially in Italy, where it has lately appeared in an Italian translation, has induced the author to republish it in a more permanent shape. He has added a considerable amount of new matter, and has entirely rewritten the section which treats of the personal infallibility of the Sovereign Pontiff. At the same time he has been careful not to depart from the original design of the work, which was to furnish laymen with a clear and succinct account, free from scholastic terms and disquisitions, of what the Church teaches with regard to her own infallibility.

THE ORATORY, LONDON,
 Feast of S. Athanasius, 1870.

TABLE OF CONTENTS.

	Page.
Infallibility lost by the Fall, and restored in the Church	1
What is meant by the word "Infallible"	8
The Subject of the Church's Infallibility :—	
1. The Pope	
2. The Pope and the Catholic Episcopate	10
The Object-Matter of the Church's Infallibility	49
1. Truths explicitly or implicitly contained in the Original Revelation	55
2 General Principles of Morality, if any, not contained in the Deposit	55
3. Dogmatic and Moral Facts	56
a. Canon and Versions of Scripture	57
b. Meaning of Books in relation to the Faith	59
c. Canonization of Saints	62
d. General Ecclesiastical Discipline and Worship	65
e. Approbation of Religious Orders	67
Condemnation of Secret and other Societies	67
g. Education	68
h. Particular Moral Facts	70
4. Political Truths and Principles	70
5. Theological Conclusions	72
6. Philosophy and Natural Sciences	75
The Way in which the Church teaches	81

CONTENTS.

	Page.
The Nature and Character of the Church's Doctrinal Condemnations ...	99
The Obligation the Church's Teaching lays on the Faithful ...	103
Exterior Obedience...	104
Interior Submission and Assent ...	105
The Object of the Assent ...	113
Obedience under Pain of Sin ...	114
Remarks on the practical bearing of the Question ...	115
Conclusion ...	124

WHEN DOES THE CHURCH SPEAK INFALLIBLY?

There is in every man a natural and instinctive craving after truth, which falsehood as such cannot satisfy. And yet, though truth is the object of the reason, so that nothing but what presents itself as truth can determine an intellectual assent, we are ever prone to mistake the counterfeit for the reality and to content the longings of our souls with cunningly-disguised falsehoods. To err is human, intellectually as well as morally.

Such was not man's state at his creation. By the gift of original justice our first parents in Paradise were incapable of forming an erroneous judgment. Though there were many things of which Adam was ignorant, he knew with absolute certainty the limits of his ignorance, and whatever he did know he knew infallibly. "It was impossible," says S. Thomas, "while the state of innocence lasted, for the understanding of the first man to acquiesce in anything false as true." (Sum. 1 qu. 94, art. 4.)

This blessed privilege of immunity from error, which, according to God's intention, would have been the inheritance of all Adam's race, was lost irrecoverably by the Fall. Man sinned in Adam, and, as a punishment of this sin, he comes into the world stripped of supernatural grace and wounded in his natural perfections. His reason, deprived of the supremacy which it exercised in the state of innocence over the inferior faculties, has lost that infallibility in its judgments which was a consequence of this supremacy. The phantasms of the imagination are now emancipated from reason's sovereignty, and falsehood finds in them the cloak of apparent truth, which alone can procure it access to the understanding. While the blind appetites of the lower nature, which the gift of original justice had enchained, so that they could not stir unless reason moved them, being now without a master, are a fresh influence at work within him to seduce his heart and lead astray his judgments. Thus by the Fall error became naturalized among mankind.

As years passed away, and Adam's children plunged deeper and deeper into sin, the darkness within grew thicker. Men lost all hold of many of the most elementary and vital truths within reason's natural sphere, or only grasped them feebly and uncertainly. The unity and personality of God, His providence, many of His attributes, the essential difference between the Creator and the creature, the moral law written on the heart of man, the spirituality and immortality of the soul, the judgment to come,—these and such-like truths were at best only realized in a partial and fragmentary way by the very sages of the heathen world. As for the multitude of men, sceptically indifferent to truths which seemed to them to rest on such uncertain foundations, they were only too ready to find a refuge from their perplexities in that practical philosophy which is so attractive to our fallen nature, "Let us eat and drink, for to-morrow we shall die" (Is. xxii. 13 ; 1 Cor. xv. 32).

Doubtless, according to the Apostle's teaching, they were "inexcusable" in this. They might have known God and His truth; "for His invisible things from the creation of the world are clearly seen, being understood by those things that are made." And it was only because they sinfully refused to know and glorify Him that "they became vain in their thoughts and their foolish heart was darkened" (Rom. i. 20, 21). Their offence, indeed, was great in thus turning their back upon the truth ; and yet they could not quite harden themselves against it, nor root out altogether the desire of it from their hearts. The superstitious practices with which their daily life was interwoven ; their belief in omens, auguries, and oracles ; the rites and ceremonies of their religious worship ; nay, even the grotesque or repulsive absurdities of their mythologies, were so many voices by which they manifested that deep and inextinguishable yearning of their souls: —Oh, that God would break the silence which encompasses Him, and would tell us what is truth !

And He, the All-merciful One, who had implanted this yearning in man's breast, was not unmindful of His creature's cry. Even at the moment when Adam stood before Him in the guilt and shame of the Fall He spoke to him, and by word of mouth and hearing of the ear told him truths of faith which he was to believe, not like natural truths on grounds of reason, but on the sole authority of Him who spoke them.

The converse which God began that day with fallen man has never since been interrupted. In every age the world has seen living exponents and heralds of God's revelation. Patriarchs and prophets have in their turn received and handed on the heavenly message. A peculiar people, chosen among the nations of the earth, was for many centuries the shrine and tabernacle of revealed truth. At length, when four thousand years had passed away, and man had proved by sad experience the depths of his ignorance and blindness, "the charity of God appeared towards us" (1 John iv. 9) in that He sent us down from heaven His "only begotten Son, full of grace and truth" (John i. 14), to be our teacher. He came, at His Father's bidding, the Uncreated Truth, the Word incarnate, and the burden of His teaching was: "I am the way, and the truth, and the life" (John xiv. 6); "For this cause came I into the world that I should bear testimony to the truth" (John xviii. 37); "If you continue in My word, you shall know the truth, and the truth shall set you free" (John viii. 32). His mission was to be Himself our light. In Him, as members of "His body which is the Church" (Col. i. 24), we were to receive back again the fulness of that truth of which sin had robbed us. The power to discern infallibly truth from error which we forfeited in Adam was to be once more ours; only in a new way, not by an interior inability to mistake falsehood for truth, but by the perpetual presence of an infallible teacher. These were "the good tidings of great joy," which the angel announced at Bethlehem. And thus was the prophecy of Isaias brought to pass: "The people that sat in darkness hath seen great light, and to them that sat in the region of the shadow of death light is sprung up" (Matt. iv. 16).

So long as Jesus remained on earth, He Himself in His own person filled this office of teacher towards His disciples. But when the time came for Him to depart hence, it was necessary that He should provide us with another teacher, to act as His representative, and to teach us in His name and with His authority. To this end He set up His Church, that it might be, until His return, "the pillar and ground of the truth" (1 Tim. iii. 15), and He "built it upon the foundation of the Apostles and prophets," He Himself being its "chief corner stone" (Eph. ii. 20). To the Church's guardianship He intrusted "the deposit" of the faith (1 Tim. vi. 20), that body of truth which He had come down from heaven to reveal. And He bade all who owned Him for their master "to hear the Church" in what she taught, under pain, if disobedient, of being regarded by their brethren "as the heathen and the publican" (Matt. xviii. 17).

For eighteen hundred years the Church has faithfully fulfilled her mission as the witness and teacher of the truth. Never once during this long period has her voice faltered or her testimony varied. No sophisms of error have perplexed her. No power of earth has overawed her. No assaults from within or from without have made her waver. No emergencies but have found her equal to them. All things have changed around her, but she has remained unchanged. Calm in the consciousness of her infallibility, as one whose eyes are ever gazing on eternal things and whose ears are always open to the harmonies of heaven, she has never ceased "to preach the word, being instant in season and out of season, reproving, entreating, rebuking in all patience and doctrine"

(2 Tim. iv. 2). From her lips, as from a fountain whose source is in the throne of God, words of truth have ever flowed. No one has sought guidance from her in vain. No one following her has gone astray. Hence the devotion which her children feel towards her. Hence the hatred with which God's enemies, be they men or devils, pursue her.

But it is only with the Church as teacher that we are now concerned. Great and manifold as are her other excellences, we must pass them by as not directly connected with the subject which we are considering. And yet, while we do this, we cannot and may not, at least with safety to ourselves, forget them altogether. The remembrance of all that the Church is, and the relation in which we stand to her, ought to affect us powerfully throughout the whole course of our inquiries,—not indeed as rendering us careless about the truth, but as inspiring us with reverential feelings in the pursuit of it. The thought that the Church is the spouse of Christ, the temple of the Holy Ghost, and our spiritual mother, will keep us from a carping and hostile spirit, as though to cut down as much as possible our mother's prerogatives could be our gain. It will hinder us from bearing ourselves towards her as slaves towards their mistress, whom they dare not disobey, but whose yoke they would evade as far as possible. Far from us be a spirit like this. We are the children of the Church. This is our glory and our liberty. And it is as the Church's loyal-hearted children that we will now draw nigh, to learn from her maternal lips the nature of the powers with which her Lord invested her, when He made her the infallible herald of His truth to generation after generation until the end.

The Church, then, is our living, ever-present, infallible teacher, charged by our Lord Himself to teach us in His name and with His authority all things necessary to our eternal salvation. This is our point of departure; and we shall assume without proof the truth of this proposition, because we are addressing Catholics, to whom it is a simple axiom of the faith. The task before us is to investigate six questions which spring out of it. In treating them, we shall have the opportunity of passing in review the principal characteristics of the Church's teaching office. These questions are as follows:—

1. What is meant by the word infallible, when we speak of the Church as our infallible teacher?

2. What is the subject of the Church's infallibility as teacher—*i. e.*, in what person or persons does her gift of teaching with infallibility reside?

3. What is the object-matter of her infallibility—*i. e.*, what precisely is the sphere within which she teaches infallibly?

4. In what way does she exercise her office as teacher?

5. What are the nature and character of her doctrinal condemnations?

6. What obligation does her teaching lay upon the faithful?

We will consider these questions in succession, adding in conclusion a few remarks on the practical bearing and importance of the whole subject.

I.

What is meant by the word infallible, when we speak of the Church as our infallible teacher? This is the first question we have to consider; and the answer is so obvious that we almost need to apologize for dwelling upon it.

To be infallible, in the ordinary acceptation of the word, is simply to be exempt from the liability to err. When, then, we say that God has made His Church infallible in her capacity of teacher, we mean that He has promised to secure her, as often as she teaches, from the possibility of declaring error to be truth and truth error. The way in which He effects this is by His supernatural providence, and the exterior guidance of His Holy Spirit. And from this point of view, infallibility is to be distinguished from the gift of inspiration. The infallible teacher, as such, receives no interior revelations or suggestions from God. The Holy Ghost does not dictate to him what to say. It is only his external utterances which are overruled, so that he cannot in his official character teach the faithful anything at variance with the truth. This distinction between infallibility and inspiration is a sufficient answer to those who object to the infallibility of the Sovereign Pontiff, that if he is infallible he must be inspired, which no theologian of any school ever asserted that he was.

Equally groundless is another argument brought against the Pope's infallibility,—that this gift necessarily implies sinlessness in its possessor, and since the Popes are not sinless, they cannot be infallible. The objection rests partly on the misuse of the word infallibility for impeccability, just as if these were equivalent in meaning, and partly on the tacit assumption that God could not with propriety guarantee from error in teaching one who, at the very time he taught, was, perchance, in sin, and therefore God's open enemy. Nevertheless, the whole economy of God's dealings with us in the order of grace is a witness to the groundlessness of this assumption. Even the least instructed Catholic knows well that sin in God's ministers is no bar to their being His instruments in the conveyance of grace to others. Every mass he hears, and every sacrament he receives, reminds him of this elementary truth. Thus the very analogy of the faith prepares us to expect that a state of grace is not a necessary condition that the divinely-appointed teacher may teach infallibly. Moreover, the Holy Scripture furnishes us with instances of the higher gift of inspiration being exercised by sinners, even when they were in the act of offending God. The prophet Balaam, moved by covetousness, sought three distinct times to pronounce a solemn curse upon Israel, but in vain, for he had "no power to speak any other thing than that which God put into his mouth" (Numbers xxii. 38). And when Caiaphas told the Jews, who were plotting our Lord's death, that they "knew nothing, and did not consider that it was expedient for them that one man should die for the people, and that the whole nation perish not," the Evangelist remarks on this, that "he spoke not of himself, but, being the high priest of that year, prophesied that Jesus should die for the nation; and not only for the nation, but to gather together in one the children of God that are dispersed" (John xi. 49-52).

If, then, the higher gift of inspiration is independent of sanctity in its possessor, how much more the lower and external gift of infallibility. In truth, these objections rest upon a half-conscious assumption that the Church's infallibility is the result of the wisdom, holiness, and prudence of her rulers, and is therefore at bottom a purely natural endowment; whereas, on the contrary, the sole ground of her inability to teach error is to be sought in the supernatural assistance and overruling guidance of the Holy Ghost, which her Divine Founder promised to her.

II.

We come now to the second question: What is the subject of the Church's infallibility—*i.e.*, in what person or persons does her gift of teaching with infallibility reside? Clearly it must reside either in the whole body of the faithful indeterminately, or it must be the exclusive property of some member or members of the body. The former alternative we may at once dismiss, for no one has ever dreamed of claiming for the faithful at large the office of teaching infallibly; nor is there any ground in Scripture or Church history for such a claim. It would be, in fact, a preposterous one, and imply a confusion in thought between the Ecclesia Docens (the Church as teacher) and the Ecclesia Docta (the Church as taught). It is true, indeed, that the body of the faithful in communion with the Holy See, for that is what we mean by the Ecclesia Docta, is infallible in believing. Whatever it believes as of faith is certainly of faith, and whatever it rejects as contrary to the faith is contrary to it. There cannot be even a temporary and partial obscuration of revealed truth throughout the Church's whole extent. But the witness it thus bears to truth is of a passive kind. Its testimony must be gathered from it by others. It cannot speak and teach, from the very fact that it is everywhere diffused throughout the world. To teach must belong to the comparatively few. Besides, its very gift of indefectibility, which qualifies it to be an infallible witness to the faith, is the result of the teaching it receives. It cannot go astray from the truth, because its teachers are infallible. "Faith comes by hearing" (Rom. x. 17). As we hear, so we are bound to believe, simply and without examination; for we are bound to subject our understandings to the revealed word as soon as it is sufficiently proposed to us. The Ecclesia Docta, then (the faithful at large), is bound to hear and accept as true the teaching of the Ecclesia Docens (the Church as teacher). And being bound to this, its only security from error lies in the infallibility of its teachers. Thus the teaching office of the Church must be vested, not in the general body, but in the few. And the infallibility which is the essential characteristic of the teaching office must belong to them independently of the taught, and be a special gift bestowed on them from above. This exactly agrees with what St. Paul would have prepared us to expect when he says that Christ "gave some apostles, and some prophets, and other some evangelists, and other some pastors and doctors, for the perfecting of the saints, for the work of the ministry, and for the building up of the body of Christ" (Eph. iv. 11, 12).

What then is the nature of this teaching body, and of

whom is it composed? In other words, who are the pastors of the Church to whom our blessed Lord has delegated the office and duty of instructing the faithful in His truth? This is what we have now to ascertain.

If we look at the beginnings of the Church as sketched out in the Gospel narrative, we are met by two independent series of facts which form the key by which to explain her subsequent organization and history. The first series relates to Peter only, and the second to the whole company of the Apostles, Peter of course included. We will consider the scope and meaning of each separately.

To begin with the passages which refer to Peter only. We read in S. Matthew's gospel, that when "Jesus came into the quarters of Cæsarea Philippi, He asked His disciples, saying: Whom do men say that the Son of man is?" The question was put to all the Apostles, and all were ready with an answer to it. "They said: Some John the Baptist, and others Elias, and others Jeremias or one of the prophets." Then once more addressing all the Apostles, "Jesus saith to them: But whom do you say that I am?" They had all replied readily to the question, "Whom do men say that the Son of man is?"; but they were silent when interrogated, "Whom do you say that I am?"—all except Peter. "Simon Peter answered and said: Thou art Christ, the Son of the living God." Hitherto our Lord had spoken to all the Apostles. He now turns to that Apostle only who, alone among his brethren, had burst forth into an open profession of belief in Christ's divinity. "And Jesus answering, said to him: Blessed art thou, Simon Bar-Jona: because flesh and blood hath not revealed it to thee, but My Father who is in Heaven. And I say to thee:" "that is," in S. Leo's paraphrase, "as My Father has manifested to thee My divinity, so I also make known to thee thy pre-eminence." "Thou art Peter:"—"that is," as S. Leo continues, "whereas I am the inviolable rock; I am the cornerstone which maketh both one; I am the foundation, other than which no man can lay; thou also art the rock, because thou art made stable through My might, so that whatever in power belongs to Me as My own is thine in common with Me by participation" (S. Leo I. in *Anniversario Assumptionis*, serm. iv.). "And I say to thee: Thou art Peter, and upon this rock I will build My Church, and the gates of hell shall not prevail against it. And I will give to thee the keys of the kingdom of heaven. And whatsoever thou shalt bind on earth shall be bound also in heaven; and whatsoever thou shalt loose on earth, it shall be loosed also in heaven" (Matt. xvi. 13—19). In these words our Lord promises to build His Church on Peter, as on a rock or immovable foundation; and He adds that, in consequence of this, the gates of hell, or Satan and his legions, shall never overthrow it. The meaning of the metaphor is obvious. As the stability of a house depends upon the stability of the ground on which it stands, so the Church is to derive its immovableness from its foundation, Peter. Thus our Lord virtually promises that Peter, on whom the whole Church is to depend, shall be himself immovable, as his new name, Peter, or Rock, imports.

But what is precisely meant by the Church being immovable, and in what way does Peter confer upon it this immovableness, and so secure it against the possibility of being overthrown? The profession of the one true faith is the condition of the Church's life, and in the unbroken continuance of this profession the Church's perpetuity consists. If Satan could succeed in corrupting the faith in one point only, he would prevail against the Church, which our Lord has promised that he shall never do. Now if the Church's indefectibility in the faith comes from Peter, so that, separate from Peter, it might err in the faith, and one with him it cannot err, this can only mean that it has in Peter's faith an unerring rule of faith, and in Peter's teaching an infallible guide, by following which with absolute interior submission, it cannot possibly stray from the faith and perish. Thus the promise of our Lord, that He would build His Church on Peter, and that the gates of hell should never prevail against it, contains, by direct implication, the further promise of Peter's infallibility. The words which follow confirm and amplify Peter's prerogatives. The keys of the kingdom of heaven, or of the Church, which Christ promised to Peter, symbolize the plenary authority and supreme jurisdiction with which he is to be invested. They show that Peter is not only to be the unerring teacher of the faith to the whole Church, but that he will have full authority to bind the faithful, under pain of exclusion from the heavenly kingdom, to conform their judgments to his teaching.

We may now pass on to the next passage, in which Peter is once more singled out by Christ from among the other Apostles, and a promise is made to him alone, in which they were to have no share. It was on the evening before the Passion that this took place. The Apostles were all gathered together round our Lord, when He began again to discourse to them about His Church, under the figure of a kingdom, which He was "disposing for them," in which they should "sit on thrones judging the twelve tribes of Israel." Thus far His words were directed to all the Apostles. But now, turning to Peter, He forewarned him, in solemn accents, of the trials which were impending over him and his brethren, the future rulers of the Church. "Simon, Simon: Behold Satan hath desired to have you, that he may sift you as wheat." You, the Apostles,—to paraphrase our Lord's words;—you, whom I have appointed to "sit on thrones judging the twelve tribes of Israel," will be tried and proved by Satan, as wheat is tossed about when it is winnowed. You, the Church's teachers, will be the special mark for Satan's wiles and assaults; for he well knows that the surest way to pervert the disciple is to corrupt the master, and that the gates of hell will prevail against the Church if he can lead astray from the faith you who are the guides and rulers of the faithful.

Such was the peril which our Lord foretold to Peter; but how did He provide against this danger, and secure the teachers of the Church from falling into errors against the faith, and thus dragging down the whole body of the faithful to perdition? "Simon, Simon: Behold Satan has desired to have *you* that he may sift *you* as wheat; but I have prayed for *thee* that *thy* faith fail not, and *thou*, being once converted, confirm thy brethren" (Luke xxii. 32). Christ's prayer carries with it its own accomplishment. When He prayed that Peter's faith might not fail, He thereby rendered Peter indefectible in the faith. And if He had offered the same prayer for all the Church's teachers, He would have secured the faith of all from the possibility of failing. But He was not pleased to do this. He prayed for Peter only. Why? Because He had already chosen Peter to be the rock on which He would build His Church, and He had made dependence on Peter's teaching the condition of His Church's stability against all the assaults of Satan. Therefore it was that He now prayed for Peter only that his faith might not fail, and He charged Peter, in virtue of that infallibility which He had impetrated for him, " to confirm his brethren "; that is, to be as a pillar of strength on which those who shared with him the office of teacher and ruler of the faithful might rest securely. Thus our Lord provided sufficiently for all the Church's needs, and yet in such a way as to mark clearly the dependence in which He willed that all the Church's members, teachers and taught alike, should stand to Peter. He made Peter stable and infallible in himself; and He promised Peter's brethren a like stability and infallibility; not, however, in themselves, but on the condition of their conforming their faith to Peter's faith, and their teaching to Peter's teaching, and so sharing by derivation in the stability and infallibility which were proper to Peter only. "In Peter therefore," to quote again S. Leo, "the strength of all is guaranteed, and the aid of divine grace is in such wise ordered, that the stability which Christ gives to Peter is conferred by Peter upon the Apostles" (Ibid.).

The promises which our Lord made to Peter on the two occasions which we have been considering referred to a time still future. We have now to see these promises accomplished, and Peter invested with the office and dignity for which he had been chosen. On one of the forty days between the Resurrection and Ascension, Jesus showed Himself to His disciples on the shore of the lake of Tiberias. "There were then together Simon Peter, and Thomas, who is called Didymus, and Nathaniel, who was of Cana, in Galilee, and the sons of Zebedee, and two others of His disciples. When, therefore, they had dined, Jesus saith to Simon Peter: Simon, son of John, lovest thou Me more than these? He saith to Him: Yea, Lord, Thou knowest that I love Thee. He saith to him: Feed My lambs. He saith to him again: Simon, son of John, lovest thou Me? He saith to Him: Yea, Lord, Thou knowest that I love Thee. He saith to him: Feed my lambs. He said to him the third time: Simon, son of John, lovest thou Me? Peter was grieved, because He had said to him the third time, Lovest thou Me? And he said to Him: Lord, Thou knowest all things; Thou knowest that I love Thee. He said to him: Feed My sheep" (John xxi. 2, 15-17).

Thus it was that the Good Shepherd, who had just before laid down His life for His sheep, when about to leave this world and return to His Father, appointed Peter to take His place on earth, and to be in His stead and with His authority the one shepherd over the one flock. Feed, or, as the word may be more accurately rendered, be the shepherd and pastor of My lambs and of My sheep. Such was Peter's commission. All who belong to the flock of Christ, Apostles, bishops, even the Mother of God herself, were placed by Christ under Peter's pastoral care, and were subjected to his supreme jurisdiction. And as "sheep follow" the shepherd, because they know his voice; but a stranger they will not follow, because they know not the voice of strangers" (John x. 4, 5), even so the sheep of Christ know and follow the voice of Peter, because in Peter's voice they hear the voice of Christ. In this way He who promised to build His Church on Peter has fulfilled His promise by constituting Peter the supreme pastor of the universal flock; at once "the pastor and the stone of Israel" (Genesis xlix. 24).

One chief portion of a shepherd's office is to provide the sheep with good and suitable food, and to keep them at a distance from all unsound and poisonous pasturages. Our Lord alluded to this when He said to Peter: "Feed My sheep." Now as the end of earthly food is to nourish and sustain the life of the body, so in like manner the food with which Peter was commanded to feed Christ's flock must consist of whatever is adapted to support the spiritual life of the sheep. But faith, according to the Apostle, is the foundation of the Christian's spiritual life, since "the just man lives by faith" (Rom. i. 17), and "without faith it is impossible to please God" (Heb. xi. 6). It therefore belongs to Peter's office, as pastor of the universal Church, to "nourish up" the sheep "in the words of faith and of good doctrine" (1 Tim. iv. 6); and to keep them from being "led away with various and strange doctrines" (Heb. xiii. 9), "contrary to the doctrine which" they "had learnt" (Rom. xvi. 17). To be able to do this, Peter must have received from Christ power to discern infallibly between what is in harmony with the faith and what is in contradiction to it. For a subordinate pastor, who has charge of only a portion of Christ's flock, may err without detriment to the whole flock, since the supreme pastor is at hand to set him right, and to warn the flock against his doctrine. But if the pastor of pastors, the shepherd of all Christ's sheep, could by any possibility teach falsehood instead of truth, since he has no superior to correct him, and as the whole flock is bound to believe according to his teaching, the Church might fall from the faith, and the gates of hell prevail against it. Hence the gift of infallibility is necessarily involved in the office of universal pastor, and, even if Christ had not already expressly promised Peter that his faith should never fail, we might have inferred his infallibility from the nature of the charge conferred upon him by the words: "Feed My lambs, Feed My sheep."

We will now turn to the passages in the Gospels which speak of special powers granted by our Lord to the whole body of the Apostles, including Peter. They are three in number. The first of these passages relates to what took place on a certain occasion during the time of our Lord's public ministry. He had been just before speaking of the way in which disobedient members of the Church were to be regarded by the faithful: "If he will not hear the Church, let him be to thee as the heathen and the publican." Then, addressing His Apostles, He continued: "Amen, I say to you, whatsoever ye shall bind upon earth shall be bound in heaven; and whatsoever ye shall loose upon earth shall be loosed in heaven" (Matt. xviii. 17, 18). These words contain a promise of universal jurisdiction over the whole Church to be conferred hereafter upon the Apostles. They are the very same words in which a similar promise was made to Peter apart from the other Apostles, when Christ chose him to be the rock on which He would one day build His Church. There is, however, this difference observable: in Peter's case they followed immediately upon the promise, "I will give thee the keys of the kingdom of heaven," and are to be referred to it, while, as spoken to the Apostles, they stand alone and without allusion to any promise of the keys. The custody of the keys, as well as the use of them, were given to Peter by himself. The use of the keys only was given to the Apostles, including Peter. From this we may gather that though the other Apostles were equal to Peter, as regards the extent of their jurisdiction, they were subordinate to him in the exercise of it. Their powers were always limited by his supremacy.

We pass on to the next passage. On the evening of the first Easter day, when "the disciples were assembled together" with closed doors "for fear of the Jews, Jesus came and stood in the midst, and said: 'Peace be unto you. As the Father hath sent Me, I also send you.' When He had said this, He breathed on them and said to them: 'Receive ye the Holy Ghost: whose sins you shall forgive, they are forgiven them; and whose sins you shall retain, they are retained" (John xx. 19, 21-23).

The third passage is as follows: on the day of our Lord's Ascension, just as He was about to leave this earth, He gave "the eleven" their mission, saying: "All power is given to Me in heaven and in earth. Going therefore, teach ye all nations, baptizing them in the name of the Father, and of the Son, and of the Holy Ghost: teaching them to observe all things whatsoever I have commanded you: and behold I am with you all days, even to the consummation of the world" (Matt. xxviii. 18–20). "He that believeth and is baptized, shall be saved; but he that believeth not, shall be condemned" (Mark xvi. 16).

From these passages we learn that what our Lord conferred upon the whole body of the Apostles, including Peter, was universal jurisdiction, and infallibility as teachers; for the right to teach all men, and to require from all belief in their teaching under pain of eternal damnation, implies that the teachers are infallible. But these powers must be interpreted consistently with those which Peter had already received apart from the rest as his personal prerogative. That which was given to the Apostles as a body could not have revoked or limited any of Peter's powers. Hence Peter still remained the sole rock on which the Church was to be built, and from which it was to derive its stability. He was still the one supreme ruler and pastor of the sheep and lambs of Christ. He still retained the guardianship of the keys of the heavenly kingdom. His faith, for which alone Christ had prayed, still continued to be the one source of firmness in the faith to the universal Church. In a word, the powers which Christ communicated to the other Apostles, as they stood before Him with Peter in their midst, did not trench upon Peter's singular and incommunicable prerogative, his supremacy. His brethren in the Apostolate never ceased to be subordinate to him in the exercise of their jurisdiction, and to depend on him as their head.

Such was in outline the organization which Christ bestowed upon His Church. He built it upon Peter, by setting up in Peter a central authority supreme, independent, and infallible; and He surrounded Peter with his brethren in the Apostolate, to aid him in his work and to share his powers, with the reserve of that on which the unity and stability of the whole Church depended, Peter's absolute and unlimited supremacy.

The early history of the Church, recorded in the Acts of the Apostles, illustrates the practical working of this organization. Everywhere we find Peter taking the lead of the other Apostles, and acting as their chief. Thus it was Peter who proposed the election of an Apostle in the place of Judas, and who addressed the assembled multitudes on the day of Pentecost. It was Peter and not John, though they were together, who cured the lame man at the Beautiful Gate of the Temple; and when the two Apostles were apprehended for preaching Christ, Peter alone spoke in defence of what had been done to the high priests and ancients of the people. At Peter's rebuke Ananias and Sapphira fell down dead, and Simon Magus trembled. The shadow of Peter passing over the sick cured them. It was Peter who, on his own authority, received into the Church the first Gentile convert, Cornelius, and thus laid down the principle which seemed so strange to the Jewish Christians; that the separation between Jew and Gentile had come to an end in Christ. When Peter was cast into prison by Herod, "prayer was made without ceasing by the Church of God for him"

(Acts xii. 5). And Paul, "three years after" his conversion, "went to Jerusalem to see Peter, and tarried with him fifteen days" (Gal. i. 18), as if to acknowledge by this external act Peter's supremacy.

At the same time we do not find that the action of the other Apostles was in any way checked or superseded by Peter; on the contrary, when great differences of opinion had arisen in the Church with regard to the obligation of the Jewish rite of circumcision upon the Gentile converts, Peter did not think fit to settle the question by an act of supreme authority, as he could have done, but "the Apostles and ancients assembled to consider of this matter" (Acts xv. 6). At length, "when there had been much disputing, Peter, rising up," gave his decision, saying, "Men and brethren, you know that in former days God made choice among us, that by my mouth the Gentiles should hear the word of the Gospel and believe. Now, therefore, why tempt ye God, to put a yoke upon the neck of the disciples which neither our fathers nor we have been able to bear?" When Peter had finished speaking, the disputing was at end, "and all the multitude held their peace," and the decision of the Apostles and the ancients was in conformity with that which Peter had indicated to them. Thus we see Peter deciding a point of doctrine; not, however, by himself, as he did when he received Cornelius into the Church, but in the midst of his brethren, their voices mingling with his in one common utterance, and possessing in union with him one common infallibility.

Such was the Church's organization during the lifetime of the Apostles. We must now consider how far it may have been modified in consequence of their death, and what portion of their powers survived them as belonging to the ordinary and permanent constitution of the Church.

The work which the Apostles were called to do was of two kinds. One part of it had reference to the establishment and first beginnings of the Church; the other part was similar to that which the Church's rulers in every age have to perform. The powers which Christ gave to the Apostles corresponded to their work, and were therefore both ordinary and extraordinary; but with this difference, that the extraordinary powers died with them, while the ordinary ones were transmitted to their successors.

If we look at Peter's powers from this point of view, we shall see that they were all ordinary. The Church was built on Peter, that it might be one; Peter was made infallible in teaching, that the Church's faith might be one; and the whole flock was intrusted to Peter's supreme rule that it might be one. The unity of the Church was the motive of Peter's supremacy, and the unity of the faith was the reason of Peter's infallibility. But if the gates of hell are not to prevail against the Church, the unity of the Church and of the faith must continue unbroken unto the end. And since Peter could secure this unity so long only as he remained on earth, at Peter's death his powers must have passed on unchanged and undiminished to his successor and heir. Hence when Christ said to Peter "On this rock, I will build My Church: I have prayed for thee that thy faith fail not, and thou being converted confirm thy brethren: feed My lambs; feed My sheep," He spoke in Peter to all Peter's successors, whom He regarded as one person morally with Peter. And as the sovereign of a kingdom never dies, though king follows king upon the throne, so likewise in Christ's heavenly kingdom upon earth, the Holy Catholic Church, Peter dies not, but lives, rules, and teaches through each successive Pontiff who in turn occupies his chair. "Peter has spoken by the voice of Leo," exclaimed the Fathers at Chalcedon (A.D. 451) when the letter of S. Leo I. was read to them. "Peter has spoken by the mouth of Pius," was the cry of the assembled bishops, on S. Peter's day, at Rome, in 1867. Fourteen centuries separated these events, and yet on both occasions the same sentiments burst spontaneously from the lips of the pastors of the unchanging and unchangeable Church, when Peter's successor addressed them.

All Peter's powers, as head and teacher of the Church, passed at his death to the next occupant of the see of Rome, and they were thenceforth indissolubly attached to this bishopric. But it was not thus with the other Apostles. Their work was extraordinary. They had to bear testimony, as eye-witnesses, to Christ's resurrection; to preach the gospel to all nations, and to found the Church in every land. When they died, their work was done; and their office, with the powers required for it, died with them. No one ever claimed to succeed them in their Apostolate, or in the infallibility and universal jurisdiction with which they were individually invested. The place they occupied in the Church was the filling of a temporary need, and others, their inferiors in dignity and jurisdiction, could carry on the work which they had begun.

The individual Apostles, with the exception of Peter,

left no one to succeed them. Bishops, indeed, are called in ecclesiastical language the successors of the Apostles, but it is because of the episcopal character which the sacrament of Holy Orders has stamped upon them, and not in virtue of their jurisdiction. Since the Apostles died, the Roman Pontiff, the occupant of the Apostolic See, is the sole Apostle in the Church. This is evident when we compare the jurisdiction of the Apostles with that enjoyed by any bishop of the Church, however widely his authority may extend. Bishops receive their jurisdiction through the Pope, who assigns to each such portion of Christ's flock as he sees fit; the Apostles received theirs from Christ Himself, and their pastoral solicitude embraced the universal Church (2 Cor. xi. 28). Bishops can be removed from their office by the Pope; the Apostles were irremovable. The jurisdiction of bishops is limited or enlarged according to the Pope's pleasure; that of the Apostles was unlimited, except by the necessary subordination to Peter, which was involved in his supremacy. Bishops are subordinate judges, from whose fallible sentences in matters of faith an appeal lies to Peter's infallible tribunal; the Apostles, being individually infallible, judged without appeal. There is, in fact, no parity between the position of individual bishops and that of the Apostles; bishops occupy a place far below the Apostles in the hierarchy of jurisdiction.

The commission which our Lord gave to the Apostles as they stood round Peter on Mount Olivet, " Going teach ye all nations whatsoever I have commanded you," was not directed merely to the individual Apostles who were then before Him, but in them to a continuing body of teachers with whom He promised to abide uninterruptedly in the exercise of their office until the end of the world. The concluding words show this: "Behold I am with you all days even unto the consummation of the world." These teachers can be none other than the bishops in communion with the Holy See; for their position in the Church's organization is permanent and indestructible; and while they derive their jurisdiction from the Sovereign Pontiff, they do not teach their flocks as his delegates, but with an authority inherent to their office. It cannot, however, have been individual bishops, in their individual capacity, whom our Lord had in view when He spoke thus; for His words bestowed universal jurisdiction and infallibility in teaching on those whom He addressed: " Teach all nations"; " I am with you." And individual bishops have only a limited jurisdiction, and are liable to err in their teaching. It was, then, to the bishops of the Church in their corporate capacity, as members of one body and acting in subordination to their one head, that He gave this commission and made this promise. As such, they are infallible, not by any personal gift, such as that which belongs to Peter's successor, but in virtue of their union with the centre of unity and ground of truth, the rock of Peter. And this infallibility the Catholic Episcopate cannot lose, because, as a whole, it cannot sever itself from Peter's Chair. The promises of Christ forbid the possibility of such a separation.

For if the bishops of the Church, as a whole, could teach anything contrary to the teaching of the Roman Pontiff, the Church would thereby cease to be built on Peter. But this cannot be; since God's overruling Providence is pledged to hinder it. To put the case of such an event happening, as is sometimes done to perplex the unwary, is an absurdity; for it is like asking what would happen if God were to contradict Himself and prove unfaithful to His promises. The maxim of S. Ambrose, "ubi Petrus ibi ecclesia," "where Peter is there the Church is," holds true, not only because the Church is bound to follow Peter, but because it cannot do otherwise than follow him. The Church under Peter is one organized body, of which Peter is the head and the faithful are the members. And since it is a body which cannot cease to exist, which it would do if the head were parted from the members or the members from the head, it follows that the members, as a whole, can never separate themselves from the Chair of Peter, or be found even for a moment in opposition to Peter's teaching. He who gave Peter the charge of His universal flock will take care that the flock, as a whole, will always obey Peter's voice, even though the enemy succeed from time to time in leading portions of it astray into the by-paths of heresy and schism.

In this sense, then, our Lord's words to the Apostles on Mount Olivet will always find their accomplishment in the Church. And it is true to say that though the Apostles, excepting Peter, have left behind them no individual successors, the Catholic Episcopate, as a whole, whether assembled in Œcumenical Council under the Pope or dispersed throughout the world in subordination to him, is the successor of the Apostles and the inheritor of apostolic powers.

We must now pass on to consider how far what we have just laid down is binding upon our assent as

Catholics. It is an article of the faith, as every one must admit, that whatever the Sovereign Pontiff and the bishops of the whole Church, acting together, teach as obligatory upon the belief of the faithful, is necessarily true. It matters not whether the Pope pronounces a dogmatic decree with the approbation of an Œcumenical Council, according to the customary phrase used on such occasions, or with the assent of the Catholic Episcopate dispersed throughout the world, every one who claims to be a Catholic must allow that pronouncements of this kind are infallible. To deny it would be to deny that the Church can teach infallibly; for if the Pope and the Episcopate together are not infallible in what they decree, where else shall we look to find infallibility?

No Catholic, then, can deny, without the guilt of formal heresy, that all dogmatic decrees of the Sovereign Pontiff, which have received the approbation of the Catholic Episcopate, are infallible. But is he equally bound to believe that the approbation of the Episcopate is a necessary and indispensable condition of this infallibility? In other words, is he required to hold that the Pope, apart from the Episcopate, is personally infallible, whenever of his own authority he pronounces a dogmatic judgment, and requires the whole Church, bishops and faithful alike, under pain of grave sin, to assent to it unreservedly?

To answer this question, we may observe that it is one thing to be bound to act upon a doctrine as true, and another to be obliged to assent intellectually to its truth. Now, putting aside for a moment the question whether it is the duty of a Catholic to hold theoretically the doctrine of the Pope's personal infallibility, there can be no doubt that he is bound, and always was bound, to hold it practically. Throughout the long course of eighteen centuries, not a single instance can be adduced of any one, whether bishop or layman, having refused submission to a dogmatic decree of the Sovereign Pontiff without being looked upon in consequence as guilty of grave sin. The excommunication usually fulminated against the disobedient is a proof of this. Never once have the Popes recognized the existence of any higher tribunal than their own. They have never tolerated any refusal to submit, on the part of the faithful, when once they had passed sentence. Nor has any one, except those whose doctrines were condemned, protested against this as a tyranny. Even Œcumenical Councils, so far from arrogating to themselves superiority over the Pope, accepted the definitions of faith which he imposed on them, as S. Leo I. did on the Fathers at Chalcedon, and humbly prayed him to confirm their decrees; thus acknowledging that these were without force until the Sovereign Pontiff had sealed them with his sanction.

The appeals from the Pope's judgment to a future General Council, which we first meet with in the fifteenth century, prove, by their novelty, how contrary to the tradition of fourteen hundred years was the doctrine of the superiority of a General Council to the Pope. There had been rebellious men in every age, but till then it had occurred to no one to cover his rebellion by such a pretext. The prompt condemnation, however, which these appeals drew down upon their authors, only served to bring home to others more vividly the practical obligation all were under to submit without reserve to the enactments of Christ's Vicar. Thus Martin V., immediately after his election (A.D. 1418), issued a bull declaring that "it is unlawful for any one to appeal from the supreme judge, namely, the Apostolic See, or the Roman Pontiff, the Vicar of Christ upon earth, or to decline his judgment in causes which concern the faith." Forty-one years later (A.D. 1459), Pius II., in the Bull "Execrabilis," after characterizing as "execrable and unheard of in ancient times the abuse which had grown up among men imbued with the spirit of rebellion, of appealing from the Roman Pontiff, the Vicar of Christ, to a future council, condemned such appeals, and reprobated them as erroneous and detestable," adding, moreover, a sentence of excommunication to be incurred *ipso facto* by all who should dare to interpose them. In the next century, Julius II., by the Bull "Suscepti" (A.D. 1509), confirmed the constitution of Pius II., declaring that all who should contravene it were " to be accounted as true and undoubted schismatics and unsound in the Catholic faith." The excommunication fulminated against those who appeal to a future General Council has never ceased to be in force, and it was recently repromulgated by Pius IX. in the Constitution "Apostolicæ Sedis" (A.D. 1869).

Nothing is clearer, from the whole history of the Church, than that the Sovereign Pontiffs have never tolerated any practical doubt of their infallibility on the part of the faithful, but have exacted from all the most unreserved submission to whatever they might decree. But they have gone beyond this, for they would not suffer without a protest their decrees to be judged by the bishops of the

Church, even though the judgment resulted in an act of submission. "Who has constituted you judges over Us?" Clement XI. wrote to the bishops of France (A.D. 1706), "Does it belong to inferiors to pass decrees about the authority of their superior and to examine his judgments? Ask your forefathers, and they will tell you that it is not the part of individual bishops to discuss, but to fulfil, the decrees of the Apostolic See. Assuredly if you had considered the form of Our Apostolic constitution, which was not devised by Us, but has been used by Our predecessors through a long series of ages, you would have seen that We neither asked your counsel, nor requested your suffrages, nor waited for your opinion; but We enjoined upon you obedience—that obedience, namely, which at your consecration you promised by a solemn oath to pay to the Blessed Peter, the Prince of the Apostles, and the Holy Roman Church, and Us and Our Apostolic mandates." If, then, the obedience which the subordinate pastors of Christ's flock are bound to pay to the judgments of the pastor of pastors is so unreserved that they may not even question their validity, who shall venture to assert, with the slightest shadow of probability, that the lambs of the fold,—that is, the clergy and laity,—may practically treat a dogmatic decree of the Sovereign Pontiff as fallible by refusing to submit to it with full and absolute adhesion? Surely to put the question thus is to answer it.

We have next to examine whether, from the theoretical and speculative point of view, the doctrine of the Pope's infallibility is equally binding upon the faithful; that is, whether every Catholic is under an obligation of assenting, interiorly, to the proposition which affirms that the

Sovereign Pontiff, when he teaches the Universal Church, and exacts interior submission from every member of it, is, by the overruling guidance of the Holy Ghost, secure from the possibility of error.

This seems at first sight a strange question to put, for certainly the practical obligation would appear to involve the speculative one as its logical consequence, since the only ground on which we can reasonably be bound to bring our understandings into captivity to the Pope's teaching is the assumption that he is infallible. To deny his infallibility and to admit that we must obey him as unreservedly as if he were infallible, is a palpable contradiction. It is not surprising, then, to find that for fourteen hundred years the doctrine of the Pope's infallibility was never questioned among Catholics. As every one recognized the practical obligation of obedience to the decrees of the Apostolic See, so every one held with undoubting certainty the speculative truth that the Pope was infallible. To prove this by evidence brought from the history of the Church would far exceed our limits, and to make a selection from evidence so wide-spread, varied, and abundant, would only convey a false impression of its cogency. Others have done this in treatises specially devoted to the subject. As for us, the testimony of Gerson, the Chancellor of the University of Paris, who first originated the opinion that the Pope is fallible, will suffice to show how strange and modern a doctrine it was even in the eyes of its inventor. "If I am not deceived," he writes, "before the Council of Constance (A.D. 1414), any one who should have dogmatically taught the opposite of this tradition [that, namely, of the Pope's supremacy and infallibility] would have been noted and condemned for heretical pravity" (Op., tom. ii. p. 247). It was in the unhappy times of the great schism, when the Church was divided into two and then three obediences, and when even the learned and the holy were unable to agree which of the rival claimants of the Papal dignity was the canonically elected Pope, that this error first saw the light. It took shape at the Council of Constance in the decree purporting that the Council had "received immediately from Jesus Christ authority to which every one, whatever might be his condition, even Papal, owed obedience in regard to faith and the extirpation of the present schism." This decree, which was passed before the reunion of the three obediences, and was never confirmed by Martin V. or any subsequent Pope, is destitute of all binding force, and has a mere historical value, as indicating a phase of opinion which existed among certain bishops and theologians of that day. The cause of this departure from the ancient tradition of the Church was that it seemed to offer a mode of escape from the insuperable difficulties which had hitherto prevented a return to unity, and to supply the means of reuniting the three obediences under one common head. By displacing the centre of authority which Christ had established, and attributing to the Council apart from the Pope the supremacy which belongs to the Pope alone, a tribunal was called into existence which claimed superiority over the Pope, and was therefore competent in its own eyes to end the schism by deposing, if necessary, the rival claimants and electing in their stead a Pope whom all would obey. The end indeed was good, but the means were evil. It was like the act of Oza, who, when David went to fetch the ark of God, "put forth his hand to the ark and took hold of it," because it leant on one side, and seemed about to fall (2 Kings vi. 6). And as "the indignation of the Lord was enkindled against Oza, and He struck him for his rashness, and he died there before the ark of God;" so in like manner, this pernicious doctrine, in its practical application and development, has been the occasion of innumerable evils to the Church and the ruin of a multitude of souls. The newly-elected Pope, Martin V., lost no time in proscribing this erroneous opinion by forbidding appeals to be made from the Sovereign Pontiff to a future General Council. This was equivalent to declaring, in contradiction to the decree of Constance, that a General Council is not superior in authority to the Pope. Otherwise appeals to a General Council could not have been rightfully forbidden, since it is always lawful to appeal from an inferior to a superior tribunal. In this way the Pope, without formally condemning the new error, did so virtually, as Gerson himself complained, by prohibiting the faithful to act upon it.

But it is easier to sow the seeds of unsound doctrine than to eradicate them when sown. The opinions professed at Constance to the detriment of the Papal supremacy bore their bitter fruit in the schismatical proceedings of the Council of Basle, which resulted at last in open schism and the creation of an anti-Pope (1431-1443). It was not long, however, before they met with a solemn and authoritative reprobation in the decree of the Œcumenical Council of Florence, by which the great Eastern schism was healed, and the Churches of the East returned to the obedience of Christ's Vicar and the unity of the faith (A.D. 1439). This decree was as follows:—

"Moreover, we define that the holy Apostolic See and the Roman Pontiff possess the primacy over the whole world, and that the Roman Pontiff himself is the successor of S. Peter, the prince of the Apostles, and that he is the true Vicar of Christ and head of the whole Church, and the father and teacher of all Christians; and that to him, in S. Peter, was delivered by Jesus Christ our Lord the full power of feeding, ruling, and governing the Universal Church; as also is contained in the acts of Œcumenical Councils and in the sacred canons."

These words, whose authority no Catholic can call in question, virtually imply the Pope's infallibility. For if the Sovereign Pontiff has received full power from Christ to teach all Christians, as the Catholic faith declares that he has, Christ's sheep are bound in conscience to believe what he teaches them, and to regard as certainly pernicious those pastures which he condemns as poisonous. But if it were possible for him to mistake falsehood for truth, and in his pronouncements to the Church to declare true doctrines to be false and worthy of censure, Christians would be bound, by God's command, to believe as truth what perchance is error, and to bring their understandings into captivity to a rule of faith which they know may be erroneous. God would thus have obliged His creatures, under pain of sin, to believe a lie; in other words, He would have contradicted His essential truth and sanctity, which is impossible. If, then, He has given us a Pastor and commanded us to believe this Pastor's teaching, it is clear that He must have pledged Himself so to guide our Pastor that he can teach us nothing but the truth.

Such, indeed, had been the instinctive reasoning of Christians from the earliest times, and such has ever continued to be the undoubting belief of the vast majority of Christians. But the new doctrines, which Gerson had devised and proclaimed at Constance, still found partisans in the country of their birth. They took root especially in the Parliaments and among the lawyers of France, who thenceforth regarded them as fundamental principles of law, and did not hesitate to push them to their practical consequences of ill-disguised rebellion against the Holy See, whenever some passing temporal advantage could be gained by it. Though adopted by the French clergy in a milder form, and held by them with less logical consistency, their effects were soon manifested in the persistent attempt to create for the Gallican Church an exceptional position in Christendom, by withdrawing it in various matters of discipline from the full control of the Apostolic See. The necessary consequence of this was, that the Church of France, so far as her strivings after independence succeeded, simply changed masters. The rulers of the State seized for themselves what was denied the Pope. The Gallican liberties, as they were called, became for the French Church bonds of servitude. As was to be expected, the kings and statesmen of France looked with favour upon a doctrine which brought such an accession of power to their hands, and furnished them with so convenient a weapon, whenever ambition or worldly policy led them to take up a position of coldness or hostility towards the Holy See.

It would, however, be unjust to the Church of France, which has been so illustrious in the Christian annals for its faith and deeds of charity, to let it be supposed that the majority of its clergy always held opinions derogatory to the Papal supremacy and infallibility. The great theological school of the Sorbonne, during the first half, at least, of the seventeenth century, was opposed to these tenets, and it was only by the compulsion of the civil power that it at last introduced them into its obligatory teaching. The same may be said of the French Episcopate, as is testified by the letter of thanks which the bishops of France addressed to Innocent X. in 1653, on his condemnation of the five propositions of Jansenius, and in which they lay down that "judgments for the confirmation of the rule of faith, pronounced by the Sovereign Pontiffs, when consulted by bishops, rest upon a divine and supreme authority throughout the Church, to which all Christians are in duty bound to render the obedience of the mind."

Even those among the clergy who speculatively denied the Pope's infallibility, did not venture to transfer their opinions from the region of speculation to that of practice, by refusing obedience to his dogmatic decrees. Nay, more than this, many of them tried, in ways more creditable to their hearts than to their understandings, to soften down the manifest opposition between the Gallican maxims and the stream of Catholic tradition, by the help of subtle distinctions and contradictory limitations. Thus they maintained that Peter's Chair was infallible, while admitting that any occupant of that Chair might teach erroneously; as though the Chair and the occupant of the Chair were not, in the language of Christian antiquity, identical. So again, while they made the subsequent assent of the whole Episcopate to a Papal definition the condition of its infallibility, as if it belonged to Peter's brethren to confirm Peter, instead of Peter his brethren; they dared not avow that the faithful might withhold their assent to the definition, until it had been satisfactorily proved by communication with all the bishops of the world that they had accepted and approved the Pope's teaching. In like manner they declared that "*full* spiritual power resided in the Apostolic See and the successor of Peter," and yet asserted that "the exercise of the Apostolic power was to be moderated" not only "by the canons" of the Universal Church, but by "the regulations, customs, and ordinances received by the kingdom and the Church of France" (Articles of 1682); as if a power could be at once plenary and limited, full and not full. The Gallican maxims, when held in restraint by the spirit of obedience, and corrected by Catholic instincts, involved their upholders in intellectual contradictions; but when they took possession of men inclined to pride and disobedience, they led them straight into heresy and schism. The history of Jansenism, Febronianism, and Josephism is an illustration of this.

If it had not been for the fostering care of the State, Gallican doctrines would soon have disappeared from the French soil. They withered or revived according to the encouragement which the rulers of the State bestowed upon them. It was in the reign of Louis XIV., and through his direct influence, that this spirit of error reached its climax, and gave a formal and definite expression to its anti-papal sentiments. The despotic principles of Louis, which led him to concentrate in his own hands all the powers of the State, made him impatient of any authority above his own, even in the spiritual order, and stimulated him to bring the Church under his control, so far as he could do this without committing himself to open heresy or schism. Unfortunately for the king and for his people, the French bishops, who should have stood between their sovereign's ambition and the Holy See, were more or less tainted with Gallican principles; and the ties which bound them to the centre of unity being thus weakened, they were ready prepared to become the pliant instruments of the royal will. Besides which, the atmosphere of the Court, which they habitually frequented, helped still more to enervate them, and to break down their moral energy; so that, in the hour of trial, it became almost impossible for them to display that courage and independence in withstanding the king which their sacred office and duty demanded of them.

The year 1682 is memorable as the epoch at which the Gallican opinions were, for the first time since the Councils of Constance and Basle, formularized and published to the world in an official document. The occasion which led to this was an unjust claim to receive the revenues of certain vacant bishoprics in France which had been set up and enforced by Louis XIV. and resisted with Apostolic firmness by Innocent XI. While this dispute was going on, an assembly of French bishops and clergy, elected under the pressure of the king's influence, drew up and signed by his command, as a menace to the Vicar of Christ, a declaration containing four articles. The fourth of these is as follows:—" In questions of faith the principal part belongs to the Sovereign Pontiff, and his decrees concern all and singular churches; but his judgment is not irreformable unless the consent of the Church be added thereunto." This article formally denied the Pope's personal infallibility, since it made his decrees dependent for their infallibility upon the consent of the Church.

Under such circumstances, the silence of the Sovereign Pontiff would have been equivalent to a tacit admission of the truth of the Gallican doctrine. Nothing, therefore, was left for the Pope but to speak. The way in which he should do this was a matter of prudence. He might have formally defined the opposite doctrine, or he might have qualified the Gallican propositions with some special theological censure. But the circumstances of the time were difficult. The good of souls rendered it inexpedient to irritate unnecessarily a monarch so powerful and full of overbearing pride as Louis XIV., who had already shown on more than one occasion how little he shrank from heaping insults and humiliation on the Vicar of Christ. Jansenism, moreover, was rife in France; and the partisans of this heresy were ready to take advantage of any breach between the king and the Holy See. The essential point was, that the mind of the Sovereign Pontiff should be distinctly manifested, and a mark set upon the doctrine which might indicate its unsoundness, even though this was only done virtually and by implication. A more explicit condemnation was unnecessary, and might have been dangerous. Accordingly, on April 11th of the same year (1682), Innocent XI. issued a brief by which he condemned and annulled all that had taken place in the assembly of the French bishops, and declared that it was void and without effect for ever. Eight years later, Alexander VII., in the Constitution "Multiplices" (A.D. 1690), expressed his reprobation of these acts in still stronger terms, by pronouncing that—

"All and everything which had been done in the assembly of the French clergy in 1682 relative to the declaration concerning the ecclesiastical power and the four propositions therein contained, was, and ever would be, *ipso jure*, null, vain, invalid, empty, and altogether and wholly void of force and effect from the beginning; and that no one was bound to the observance of them, or any part of them, even though he had engaged himself thereunto by oath."

Later still, when the disputes between Louis XIV. and the Holy See had been arranged, the French clergy who had taken part in the Assembly of 1682, and were afterwards nominated by the king to vacant bishoprics, could not obtain from Innocent XII. their bulls of institution until they had written to the Pope in the following terms (1692):—

"Prostrate at the feet of your Holiness, we profess and declare that we grieve from our heart exceedingly and beyond what can be expressed, for the things done in the Assembly of 1682, which have excessively displeased your Holiness and your predecessors. Wherefore, whatever could have been looked upon as decreed in the aforesaid Assembly concerning the ecclesiastical power of the Pontifical authority we regard as not decreed, and we declare that it ought to be so regarded."

Even Louis XIV. seems to have felt some regret for what he had done, since he also addressed a letter to Innocent XII., in which he says:—

"That I may give you the clearest possible proof of filial dutifulness, I joyfully and gladly signify to your Holiness that I have already given the necessary orders that the decree which, impelled by circumstances, I had issued to secure the observance of the declaration of the Assembly of 1682, shall remain without effect."

Louis XIV. kept his word, and the edict, though never repealed, was not enforced during the remainder of his reign. Still the Declaration of 1682 continued, under the patronage of the Parliaments and the Court, to exercise considerable influence on the theological training of the French clergy. The Gallican maxims rooted themselves in the Sorbonne from the time that the Parliament of Paris compelled that body to enter upon its registers the Declaration of 1682; and when once these doctrines had established themselves there, they never lost their hold upon its teaching. Tournely, one of its doctors, writing in 1739, speaks of the difficulty which he found in harmonizing the passages adduced by Bellarmine, and others from Christian antiquity, with the Declaration of 1682, "from which," he adds, "we are not permitted to depart." But before the century had come to an end, a little more than a hundred years after the celebrated Declaration was published, the great Revolution swept over France, and carrying away with it the constituted order of things in Church and State, forced the French Church to turn again to the rock of Peter for defence, and to renew those more intimate relations with the Sovereign Pontiff on which the life and vigour of the Church's action so much depend.

It was in vain that Napoleon I., and after him the kings of the Restoration, sought to recall to life and put in practice the Gallican doctrines of the past. They still indeed lingered for awhile, as might have been expected, among the elder clergy, who had received their ecclesiastical training before the revolution; but they found no favour with the younger generation, whose hearts were drawn more and more by a multitude of converging influences towards the Chair of Peter. Hence it has come about that at the present day the dogma of the Pope's infallibility is nowhere more firmly believed and more enthusiastically proclaimed than in France itself. In all other parts of the Church, with some few passing exceptions due to the tyranny of the State, this doctrine has always been held as a most certain truth, theoretically no less than practically.

The Pontificate of Pius IX. will be ever glorious in the Church's annals for the way in which the acts of the Holy Father have conduced to bring into evidence and give expression to the depth and universality of the Church's belief in the infallibility of Christ's vicar. We will mention several instances in illustration of this.

In the Encyclical which Pius IX. addressed to all bishops in communion with the Apostolic See, on 9th November, 1846, soon after his elevation to the Chair of Peter, he thus expresses himself:—

"God Himself," he writes, "has constituted a living authority to teach and establish the true and legitimate sense of His heavenly revelation, and to settle by an infallible judgment all controversies in matters of faith and morals, lest the faithful be 'carried about with every wind of doctrine by the wickedness of men, according to the contrivance of error.' This living and infallible authority is to be found in that Church only which, having been built by Christ our Lord upon Peter, the head, prince, and pastor of the whole Church, whose faith He promised should never fail, has always had its legitimate Pontiffs, deducing without interruption their origin from Peter, seated in Peter's Chair, heirs and guardians of Peter's doctrine, dignity, honour, and power. And since, where Peter is, there is the Church (S. Ambros. in Psalm xl.), and Peter speaks through the Roman Pontiff (Concil. Chalced. Act 2), and always in his successors lives and exercises judgment (Synod. Ephes. Act 3), and bestows on those who seek it the truth of faith (S. Petr. Chrysol. Epist. ad Eutych.), therefore the Divine utterances are to be taken in that precise sense which was and is held by this Roman Chair of Blessed Peter, which, as the mother and teacher (*magistra*) of all the Churches (Concil. Trid. Sess. VII. de Bapt.), has ever preserved whole and inviolate the faith delivered by Christ, and has taught it to the faithful, showing to all the way of salvation and the doctrine of uncorrupted truth."

There is nothing new in this letter: for the voice of Peter is the same in every age, and "profane novelties of words" (1 Tim. vi. 20) are strangers to the Apostolic Chair. But though it declares plainly the Pope's infallibility and the obligation which lies on every Christian to yield submission to his teaching, not even a dissentient murmur was heard throughout the Church, and not a bishop so much as hinted that the Pope had gone beyond the truth in this plain assertion of his infallibility. Why was this, except that Gallicanism was at last extinct, and that the pastors and the flock, the sheep and the lambs of Christ alike, believed in their inmost hearts that the one pastor to whose care Christ had consigned them was infallible?

That which Pius IX. had taught in word at the beginning of his reign, he taught also in deed; when, on the 8th of December, 1854, "by his supreme and infallible utterance," as the sixth lection of the Feast in the Roman breviary has it, he defined that the doctrine of the Immaculate Conception of the Blessed Virgin Mary "has been revealed by God, and is therefore to be firmly and constantly held by all the faithful. Wherefore if any, which God forbid, presume in their hearts to think differently from what we have defined, let them know and be assured that they are condemned by their own judgment, have suffered shipwreck concerning the faith, and have departed from the unity of the Church." What stronger practical evidence of infallibility can we have than this? The moment before Pius IX. spoke these words, interior assent to the doctrine of the Immaculate Conception was not obligatory on the faithful. The moment after he had spoken them, none who heard him could doubt interiorly the truth of the dogma without committing a formal sin of heresy and incurring the forfeiture of their salvation. No time was given to ascertain whether the bishops of the Church everywhere accepted the Pope's judgment; and yet, on Gallican principles, this acceptation is necessary to make the judgment infallible. No half assent, no provisional submission was admissible. Pius IX. required the faithful to yield at once to the definition that absolute and unquestioning assent of the intellect which is due to a revealed dogma, and he declared that to refuse this was "to suffer shipwreck concerning the faith, and to have departed from the unity of the Church." Surely on that day Gallican doctrines were manifested to the world in their full absurdity. An opinion which cannot be acted upon without formal heresy stands self-condemned.

The publication of the Encyclical "Quanta Cura," and of the Syllabus of condemned errors (A.D. 1864), added fresh lustre to the doctrine of the Pope's infallibility, and exhibited once more how universal is the belief in it. Everywhere these documents met with unquestioning submission, and were welcomed as divine oracles. Nor did any bishop presume to judge them before accepting them, except in that way only in which, as Fénélon says, it is lawful for a bishop to judge what the Pope has decreed, namely, by conforming his judgment to that of the Pope.

Such is the history of the doctrine of the Pope's infallibility. It has been everywhere, and at all times, practically held by Catholics, and no one has ever refused submission to a doctrinal decree of the Sovereign Pontiff without forfeiting his title to be called a Catholic. On the other hand, since the Church has not yet declared by a formal and express definition that this doctrine is of faith, to deny it speculatively does not entail the guilt of heresy. But it does not follow from this, that it is an open question on which a Catholic may take which side he pleases; for there are many truths of which we may be certain, without having the highest kind of certainty concerning them—that of divine and obligatory faith. And there are doctrines which the Church, for prudential reasons, may not have seen fit to brand by a distinct sentence as heretical, but about which she has so clearly manifested her mind, that she can hardly be said to regard them even as tolerated. Such a one as we have seen, is the opinion which denies the Pope's personal infallibility. Condemned virtually again and again by the Church; repudiated by the overwhelming majority of Catholics; leading, if acted upon, to heresy and schism; opposed to the tradition and teaching of the Apostolic See; stigmatized by theologians as heretical or erroneous; unknown for fourteen centuries in the Church; begotten in times of disunion and bewilderment; nursed by lawyers and statesmen as a weapon against the Vicar of Christ; imposed on a reluctant clergy by a tyrannical king; the new-found ally of modern liberalism; illogical and self-contradictory as a system;—Gallicanism has lived ignobly and will die ignobly. A year ago it seemed an extinct thing—the relic of a past age, when suddenly, amid the plaudits of the anti-Christian press of Europe, it was galvanized into the semblance of a momentary vitality, and at once proved itself to be the same that it ever had been, by the noisy disloyalty of its behaviour towards the Apostolic See. But the times are altered. The relations of Church and State are not what they once were. Monarchs, if they have the will, have no longer the power, to shield from formal condemnation this pernicious error. Its unexpected resuscitation, and the new manifestation of its spirit and tendencies, which has astonished and scandalized the faithful, will be its death warrant. Many who might have wished it let alone, as not worth a formal condemnation, now desire, with good reason, that it may be crushed for ever. Hence it is that all eyes are fixed upon the Fathers of the Church now gathered in Œcumenical Council round the Chair of Peter at Rome, in prayerful expectation that, ere long, a decree may thence go forth relegating this evil doctrine to the outer darkness of heresy, and proclaiming as a dogma of the faith that the Roman Pontiff, the Vicar of Christ on earth, cannot err from the truth, whenever in his Master's name and authority he teaches the Universal Church.

III.

We may now pass to the third question: What is the object-matter of the Church's infallibility, *i.e.*, what precisely is the sphere within which she teaches infallibly? To reply to this question we must consult the Church herself. She is God's ambassador. She alone knows the extent of her powers. We have admitted her credentials and accepted her as God's envoy. It is therefore only reasonable that we should believe her word in what she tells us about the object and scope of her mission. Whatever she declares to be within the province of her infallibility as our teacher must be within it. If we prove that she has claimed to speak infallibly on any point, we have proved that she has spoken infallibly upon it.

Now the Church does not derive her powers from a written document. She came into existence as a living and energizing institution. There was therefore no need for her to begin by defining accurately the extent of her authority. She declared the powers which she possessed by using them. She did not define that she was infallible, but she always acted as one who could not err. Whenever unsound doctrines made their appearance she condemned them, and when truths were in danger of becoming obscured or perverted she proclaimed them anew. And though the forms which error assumes are numberless and ever changing, she has never wearied of pursuing it, in whatever field of thought or speculation it might spring up, that she might brand it at once as error and set the sheep of Christ on their guard against it. Thus, in God's providence, the course of events has served to exhibit with increasing definiteness the full extent of the Church's infallible authority as teacher and to mark out more and more accurately the field over which it ranges.

But though external circumstances have tended to place in new lights the Church's power, it would be incorrect to say that she receives fresh influxes of power from above to meet the necessities of each age as they arrive. Her authority was given her in its fulness from the first. Time only unfolded and brought out what was there already. Those in whom the power resided applied it with unerring instinct when occasions occurred calling for its exercise. We may trace it all substantially in that commission which our Blessed Lord gave to His Apostles before His Ascension. "All power," He says, "is given to Me in heaven and on earth. Going therefore, teach ye all nations, baptizing them in the Name of the Father, and of the Son, and of the Holy Ghost: teaching them to observe all things whatsoever I have commanded you, and behold I am with you all days even to the consummation of the world" (Matt. xxviii. 18, 19). These words were indeed spoken to the Apostles, and applied primarily to them. But the promise appended to the command, by which our Lord engages to be present with those whom He addressed "all days even to the consummation of the world," shows that He spoke likewise to the undying Church in the person of the Apostles, and gave her also the commission which He gave to them.

This commission to teach all nations to observe whatever our Lord had commanded the Apostles, not only expresses the charge laid upon the Church to teach, but declares in epitome and substance what was to be the matter of her teaching. Clear as this is, it becomes still clearer when we compare it with the promises which Jesus had already made to his Apostles, and in their person to the Church.

"The Paraclete, the Holy Ghost, whom the Father will send in My name, He will teach you all things and bring all things to your mind whatsoever I shall have said to you" (John xiv. 26); and again, "When He, the Spirit of Truth, shall come, He will teach you all truth" (John xvi. 13). In these words we see laid down in broad outlines how far the sphere of the Church's office as our teacher extends. "All truth," "All things whatsoever I have said to you," "whatsoever I have commanded you"—*i.e.*, the whole economy of salvation, all, namely, that men have to believe and do in order to attain eternal life, fall under the Church's authority as teacher, and therefore under her infallibility. Hence has come the common definition that the Church is infallible in all that she teaches regarding faith and morals, since faith refers to what we must believe, and morals to what we must do. And the definition is a correct one, provided care be taken to explain that by matters of faith and morals are meant not only the truths directly revealed by our Blessed Lord to His Apostles, whether explicitly or implicitly, but also every other branch of truth, speculative or practical, which has any bearing upon revealed truth. On the other hand, if the words faith and morals are so interpreted as to confine the Church's infallibility to revealed truth exclusively, the definition becomes false and dangerous. It was, in fact, by an evasion of this kind that the Jansenists endeavoured to fortify their position of rebellion against the Church. "The fundamental principle," writes Fénélon, "so much vaunted by the [Jansenist] party is false and unsustainable. This principle is that the infallibility of the Church does not extend beyond things revealed" (Instruction Pastorale sur le Silence respectueux.—Œuvres, tom. xiv. p. 46). If this principle were carried out in detail, it would be impossible, as we shall see, for the Church to fulfil her office as teacher of the truth and guide to heaven. The dogmas of faith themselves would become obscured and be in danger of perishing, if the Church could only teach infallibly truths directly and immediately contained in the revealed deposit. But this is a point about which the Vicar of Christ, Pius IX., has spoken, twice at least, quite distinctly. In the Brief "Gravissimas inter" addressed (1862) to the Archbishop of Munich, the Pope declares that "the Church, in virtue of the power intrusted to her by her Divine Author, has the right and the obligation not only of refusing to tolerate, but also of proscribing and condemning *all errors, if the integrity of the faith and the salvation of souls demand it.*" He then adds that "the opinion which teaches the contrary to this is altogether *erroneous, and in the highest degree insulting to the faith of the Church and her authority.*" Hence, since it is erroneous—that is to say, in popular language, not far off heresy—to deny the Church's right to condemn all errors affecting the integrity of the faith and the salvation of souls, it follows necessarily that the Church's infallibility as teacher extends over all truths which have a bearing upon the faith and upon the eternal welfare of mankind. Again, Pius IX. has spoken no less emphatically and clearly on this question in the Encyclical " Quanta Cura " (1864). In this document, which the Pope addressed to all the bishops of the Church, he says :—

" Nor can We pass over in silence the audacity of those who, not enduring sound doctrine, contend that ' without sin and without any sacrifice of the Catholic profession, assent and obedience may be refused *to those judgments and decrees of the Apostolic See whose object is declared to concern the Church's general good, and her rights and discipline, so only it do not touch the dogmas of faith and morals.*' But no one can be found not clearly to see and understand how grievously this is opposed to the Catholic dogma of the full power given from God by Christ our Lord Himself to the Roman Pontiff of feeding, ruling, and governing the Universal Church."

These words, it may be observed by the way, furnish an additional proof of the Sovereign Pontiff's personal infallibility. If assent cannot be refused to the Pope's judgments, without such sin as will entail the sacrifice of the Catholic profession, it is clear that he must possess the gift of infallibility in those judgments. Otherwise we might be bound, under pain of mortal sin, to believe as truth what was really false. It was not, however, for this purpose that we quoted the passage, though the remark just made was too pertinent to our subject to allow of its being omitted. We adduced the words in order to show that, in the judgment of the Sovereign Pontiff, the Church is empowered to teach not merely points of doctrine which " touch the dogmas of faith and morals " (*i. e.*, which touch them directly in the way of direct inference, for that such is the meaning is plain from the passage previously quoted from the Munich Brief), but also whatever " concerns the Church's general good and her rights and discipline."

From what has been said, it is evident that the sphere of the Church's infallible teaching is very extensive, and embraces a great many different subjects, since there can be very few branches of truth which have not some connection with revealed dogma. This, however, will appear still more clearly when we examine in detail the object-matter of her teaching office. We shall at the same time have the opportunity of observing the relation, more or less close, which the several subjects taught by her bear to the revealed deposit, and on which her right to teach infallibly concerning them is grounded.

We may now enter upon this inquiry and consider, one by one, under general heads, the matter of the Church's teaching.

1.—Truths explicitly or implicitly contained in the Original Revelation.

These truths are of two kinds. Either they are truths which we could only have known by revelation, such as the mystery of the Most Holy Trinity; or they are truths which we can arrive at naturally by the exercise of our reason, but which, by the fact of their having been revealed form part of the revealed deposit, and are thus known to us by faith as well as by reason, *e. g.*, many principles of natural religion and the moral law. These truths form the direct and primary object of the Church's infallibility. But it is needless to dwell on this head. Grant that the Church is our teacher in the faith, and it follows necessarily that she must know with unerring certainty what the revealed doctrines are which she has to teach. Besides since it is only in virtue of the Church's infallible knowledge of revealed truth that she professes to judge infallibly matters, not revealed, but indirectly connected with revelation, if she cannot determine infallibly what is contained in, or immediately deducible from, the original revelation, she has no claim to infallibility at all.

2.—General Principles of Moralty, not contained in the Deposit, but resting solely on the Authority of Reason.

It may indeed be questioned whether there are any such, for most of the principles of morality can be directly deduced from what is revealed, *e. g.*, from the Holy Scriptures. Still, supposing such to exist, they none the less fall within the province of the Church's infallibility. This arises from the indirect bearing they have upon revealed truth; since the Church could not teach doctrines contradictory to these without thereby forfeiting her sanctity, and proving herself an untrustworthy guide to the flock in matters concerning eternal salvation—a thing which revelation declares to be an impossibility. Therefore the Church, in order to be able to fulfil her office, must have power to recognize without danger of mistake, general truths of morality, even though they may not have been originally revealed.

3.—Dogmatic and Moral Facts.

Under this head may be ranged a variety of facts which the Church teaches as infallibly certain, though they are neither part of the revealed deposit nor deducible from it. She grounds her claim to do this on the relation which they bear to dogma and morals, and which is such that the knowledge of them is indispensable to the faithful in order that they may be able to learn the faith from her and to continue to hold it, as well as true principles of morality, without taint or error. But if it is necessary for the good of the faithful that they should know these facts infallibly, it is equally necessary that the Church should be infallible in pronouncing upon them. Thus it follows from the Church's office of teacher of the faith and guide to Heaven, that dogmatic and moral facts fall within the province of her infallibility.

(a.) The Church can determine infallibly the Canon of Scripture, the Authenticity of particular Versions of Scripture, and the Œcumenicity of Councils.

It would be of no use to us to know that certain books had been inspired by the Holy Ghost, unless we could be sure which these books were; nor, again, would it profit us much to be told the names of the inspired writings, unless we could be further satisfied that the copies of these writings which had come down to us were free from corruption, and contained from beginning to end nothing but the pure and unadulterated word of God.

Now the Sacred Scriptures cannot bear testimony to themselves. Their authenticity must rest on evidence external to them. The very earliest manuscripts of the New Testament do not date beyond the fourth century of the Christian era; that is, several centuries after the originals were written. The historical difficulties which have been alleged against portions of the canonical Scriptures—for example, the Apocalypse—are by no means contemptible. The whole history of Protestantism, especially in Germany, shows the perplexities with which the question of the canon is beset, for those who have substituted their own private judgment for the authority of the Church.

These considerations tend to show that, when Christ gave us in the Church an infallible teacher He must have willed that her infallibility should extend to the determination of the canon of Scriptures. It was this which made S. Augustine write:— "I should not believe the Gospel unless the authority of the Catholic Church moved me to do so " (L. cont. Epist. Fundam. c. 4). Hence we find that the faithful have always looked to the Church to tell them which were the canonical Scriptures. Thus, for example, at the beginning of the fifth century Pope Innocent I. sent to Exuperius of Toulouse a list of the sacred writings, which agrees exactly with that which was solemnly approved eleven hundred years later by the Council of Trent in the following decree:—"If any one shall not receive as sacred and canonical these books in their entirety, with all their parts, just as they are wont to be read in the Catholic Church, and are contained in the old Vulgate Latin edition, let him be anathema."

On the same grounds it is plain that the Church has power to determine infallibly whether a given text is substantially genuine, and to declare that a particular version is to be received by the faithful as authentic. Thus, the Council of Trent pronounced that "the old Vulgate edition, which has been approved by the long use of many centuries in the Church, is to be regarded in public lectures, disputations, sermons, and expositions as authentic, and that no one dare or presume under any pretext whatever to reject it." This does not mean that the Vulgate translation is faultless, but that it is free from errors of faith and morals, and that, viewed as a receptacle of revealed truths, it contains neither more nor less nor anything different from the original text.

Again, the Church can infallibly decide that a particular council must be received by the faithful as œcumenical. For example, the fifth article on which Martin V. and the Council of Constance commanded persons suspected of holding the tenets of Wickliff and Huss to be examined runs thus :—" Whether he believes, holds, and asserts that every General Council, and also the Council of Constance, represent the Universal Church?" Here assent is required to a dogma and a dogmatic fact; the dogma being that General Councils represent the whole Church, and the fact that the Council of Constance is a General Council. If the Church could not infallibly determine this fact, she could not practically enforce submission to her enactments. For the disobedient would always devise pretexts for questioning the œcumenicity of any council whose decisions were repugnant to them, and then, with seeming good conscience, refuse at least interior obedience to its decrees. But our Lord has anticipated this evasion, and so prevented Œcumenical Councils from becoming nugatory, by empowering His Church authoritatively to determine that a particular Council is œcumenical, and must be obeyed.

(b.) *The Church claims the power to determine infallibly what is the precise sense of a given book, or passage of a book; and whether this sense is or is not in conformity with revealed truth.*

Here we have a fact which cannot be said to have been originally revealed—namely, whether a particular book has or has not a certain definite sense : for example, whether a certain series of five propositions really embodies the doctrine contained in the Augustinus of Jansenius. These propositions are not verbally contained in the Augustinus, but they represent the results of a careful examination of the work, and are the fruit of painstaking study and laborious collation of the different parts of the book one with another. Hence the Jansenists argued that the fact of the five propositions being contained in the Augustinus, is in itself an essentially human fact, and that, as such, its truth is an open and fairly debatable question. For, they said, what is so difficult to ascertain precisely as the exact sense of a large book on a deep theological subject? And, if there is any point on which theologians may justly claim to be allowed to form an opinion for themselves, it is whether these five propositions represent the true meaning of the Augustinus or not. Surely this is a question utterly beyond the power of the Church, as teacher, to determine infallibly. Let her keep to the faith, and not pretend to conduct infallibly a purely critical investigation. To enforce such a pretension would be a tyrannical domineering over consciences. Such was the line of argument which the Jansenists adopted to justify their disobedience. They fully admitted that the Church had power to judge and condemn the doctrine of the five propositions, taken by themselves, but they resolutely denied her right to pass judgment upon the concrete fact that these propositions were a correct and accurate expression of the doctrine of the Augustinus. And they defended their position with the ingenuity, subtlety, and obstinacy which characterized them. On the other hand, the Church refused to tolerate for a moment this Jansenist distinction. She " declared and defined," by the mouth of the Sovereign Pontiff, Alexander VII. (1656), " that the five propositions had been extracted from the book of Cornelius Jansenius, Bishop of Ypres, entitled Augustinus, and had been condemned in the sense intended by the same Cornelius," *i.e.*, as afterwards explained, in the sense such as it could be gathered from the book itself. And still more effectually to put an end to the evasions of the Jansenists, the same Pope Alexander VII. (1665) issued the following formulary, which he required bishops and clergy to swear to and to subscribe :—

"I submit myself to the Apostolic Constitution of the Sovereign Pontiffs Innocent X., dated 31st May, 1653, and Alexander VII., dated 16th Oct., 1656, and with sincere mind I reject and condemn the five propositions extracted from the book of Cornelius Jansenius, entitled Augustinus, and I do this in the sense intended by the aforesaid author, as the Apostolic See has condemned them in the above-mentioned Constitutions, and thus I swear, so help me God and these God's holy Gospels."

In compelling the bishops and clergy to swear that they sincerely believed the five condemned propositions to be contained in the Augustinus, the Church showed most clearly that she had not the slightest doubt about her power to determine infallibly this fact, and that her children had no right in conscience to doubt her power. For if a doubt had been admissible, she could not lawfully have exacted the oath, since she would have exposed the bishops and clergy to the danger of perjuring themselves by swearing that they were absolutely certain of a fact for which they had no sufficient ground of certainty except her (on the hypothesis) fallible authority. But she knew, and with good reason, that though she had no direct power to judge this fact, in so far as it was a purely human one, indirectly she had power to decide concerning it because of its close connection with revealed dogma. For without such power it would have been impossible for her to warn her flock against poisonous pastures or to point out to them what books contain sound and wholesome doctrine: and thus virtually she would have been obliged to abdicate her office of pastor and teacher of Christ's flock. As, however, she knew well the extent of her powers, she has never hesitated in every age to condemn and proscribe unsound books. History abounds with instances of this. Thus the first Œcumenical Council, that of Nice (325), condemned the Thalia of Arius; and the Councils of Ephesus (431) and Chalcedon (451) anathematized the writings of Nestorius and Eutyches respectively. S. Leo I. again proscribed the books of the Manichees. And so it has been age after age, up to the present day, when on more than one occasion Pius IX. has condemned books by his Apostolic letters on account of the unsound doctrines which they contained. Hence, whether we look at the reason of the thing or at the constant practice of the Church from primitive times downwards, it cannot be denied that the Church, as teacher of the faith, claims and has the right to claim infallibility in determining the sense of books or passages of books, in so far as this bears upon and affects the revealed deposit of which she is the guardian.

(c.) *The Canonization of Saints.*

This, again, is an instance of a moral fact. When the Church canonizes a saint, she solemnly and officially declares to the whole body of the faithful, that the soul of the canonized saint is, as a matter of fact, in heaven, and she requires all her children to believe this. Witness, for example, the words of the decree by which Pius II. canonized S. Catherine of Siena; and the bulls of anonization of other saints, it may be remarked, are couched in similar terms :—

"By the authority of our Lord Jesus Christ and of the Blessed Peter and Paul and Our own, We declare .... that Catherine of Siena has been received into the heavenly Jerusalem, and gifted with a crown of eternal glory; and We decree and define that she is to be worshipped as a saint publicly and privately."

Moreover, the canonization of a saint is not a solitary act occurring once or twice in the course of ages. On the contrary, it has been a practice of the Church from the earliest times, and not a century passes away without a certain number of fresh canonizations. Again, in canonizing a saint, the Church does not merely permit the worship of the saint, as in the case of a beatification; but she lays it as an obligation upon multitudes of the faithful, at least in the case of those saints whose office and mass are extended to the universal Church; and this, too, not as a private act of worship, but as a part of her public and daily liturgy, since it is in her name that the mass is offered and the office recited by her clergy and religious. Now, here we have a long and continually increasing series of facts, namely, that such and such individuals are now saints in heaven, upon which the Church practically professes to decide with such infallible certainty, that she compels her priests, under pain of mortal sin, year after year on the festival days of these saints, to offer the adorable sacrifice in their honour, and her clergy and religious under the same penalty to invoke them in the

Divine office, and to recite or sing their praises in her name. And yet these facts are in no sense revealed facts, for they are simply conclusions inferred from the evidence or human testimony by which the heroicity of the virtues, the final perseverance, and the miracles of the saints have been proved.

Doubtless, the evidence adduced is so full and cogent in itself, and has been so carefully weighed and sifted, that even, humanly speaking, we have the strongest moral certainty that a canonized saint really died in grace and is in heaven. Still this does not render it any the less a human fact, nor make it obligatory on those who have not gone through the evidence to take it on trust, and submit their understanding absolutely to those who have examined it. How, then, does the Church venture to decide the question on her own authority, and to oblige her children to accept the fact as true, not on the intrinsic merits of the case, but because she has defined it? It is simply because it is so intimately connected with the first principles of faith and morals. For what could be more essentially opposed to both these than the supposition that the Church, man's divinely-appointed guide, whose note is sanctity, should oblige her children, under pain of grievous sin, publicly and in her name to invoke, worship, and offer sacrifice in honour of souls which, perchance, are among the damned? Such a supposition is repulsive to our instincts as Catholics and men. God, who wills that the saints in heaven should be our intercessors with Him, and the objects of our worship upon earth, must have given His Church power to determine infallibly which of her departed children are worthy of our homage.

(d.) Ordinances relating to general Ecclesiastical Discipline and Worship.

Pius VI., in the brief "Quod Aliquantum," addressed 10th March, 1791, to the French bishops upon the subject of the civil constitution of the clergy decreed by the National Assembly, takes occasion to remark upon "the close connection which discipline often has with dogma, and how great its influence is in maintaining the purity of dogma." He adds that Councils have frequently excommunicated those who violate discipline, and that the Council of Trent, in various places, has anathematized impugners of ecclesiastical discipline. As instances, he mentions the excommunication pronounced by the Council against all who deny that Christians are bound to communicate at Easter, as well as against those who assert that the ceremonies, vestments, and external signs used at mass are incentives to impiety, or that the practice of saying the Canon of the Mass and the words of Consecration in a low voice is to be condemned, and that Mass ought only to be celebrated in the vulgar tongue; or that the Church cannot make diriment impediments of marriage, or has erred in making them; or that clerics in holy orders or professed religious can validly contract marriage in spite of the ecclesiastical law and the vow; or that the prohibition to solemnize marriage at certain seasons of the year is a Gentile superstition; or, again, who condemn the benedictions and other ceremonies used by the Church in solemnizing nuptials; or, lastly, who assert that matrimonial causes do not belong to the ecclesiastical judges. After this enumeration, the Pope goes on to remark that, "from the fulmination of excommunication against those who assail various points of discipline we may clearly infer that discipline is regarded by the Church as connected with dogma." But this connection, according to the principles already laid down, brings the whole range of general ecclesiastical discipline within the Church's infallibility. Hence she cannot enact disciplinary laws binding upon all the faithful, which are virtually incompatible with the purity of faith and morals. Otherwise, through these laws, she would be indirectly sapping the foundations of the faith in the souls of her children, and thus fall into palpable contradiction with herself as the infallible teacher of the faith.

In like manner, whatever the Church ordains relative to public worship must be in harmony with the faith. "Lex orandi, lex credendi:" as we are bound to pray, so we are bound to believe. Thus the prayers we offer for the dead impress upon our minds, and so teach us the doctrine of purgatory. The exorcisms used in baptism bear witness to the dogma of original sin. The genuflections to the Most Holy Sacrament help us to realize Christ's real presence. The doxology, with which we terminate each psalm, reminds us of the mystery of the Ever Blessed Trinity. Hence, through the necessary connection of worship with dogma, we may infer that the sanctity of the Church and her office as teacher of the faith alike require that she should be so far infallible in regard to the worship of God that she cannot command the universal flock to adopt any forms or mode of worship virtually inconsistent with revealed truth. Consequently, the mere fact that the Roman missal, pontifical, breviary, and ritual have been formally approved by the Sovereign Pontiff, and imposed by him as of obligation upon the clergy, is proof sufficient that they contain nothing contrary to faith, morals, or piety.

(*e.*) *The Approbation of Religious Orders.*

When the Church approves a religious order, she defines and declares that the object, rule, and constitutions of the order are morally good, in harmony with the Evangelical counsels, and suitable for the attainment of Christian perfection. Here, again, we have a fact wholly exterior to the revealed deposit; and yet it is a fact upon which the Church must be empowered to pronounce infallibly if she is, as she professes to be, the teacher of the faith and our guide to heaven. For the practical consequence of a mistake on her part in approving a religious order would be to deceive her children by inducing them to embrace a mode of life which they believed, on her authority, would help them on to perfection, but which in reality would lead them away from it. As, however, the Church cannot prove an unreliable guide, it follows that she cannot err when she seals a religious order with her formal approbation.

(*f.*) *The Condemnation of Secret and other Societies.*

The object, rules, and doctrines of a society are human facts. Since, however, they must be either in harmony with, or in opposition to, the principles of the faith and morality, they become, from this point of view, dogmatic and moral facts, and, as such, are matter regarding which the Church can teach infallibly. The same reasons which prove that she is empowered to judge infallibly the doctrines of a book or the rules of a religious order, show that she must have a similar power in respect of societies. For her children need to be warned against dangers to their faith and morals in the one case quite as much as in the other. Accordingly, we find that the Church practically claims this power by forbidding the faithful to become or to continue members of particular societies, sometimes even—as in the case of the Freemasons and the Carbonari—under pain of excommunication.

(*g.*) *Education.*

There is nothing of greater consequence to the well-being of Christ's flock than that the children of the faithful should be trained up and educated in a way conformable to right faith and morals. Nor is there any surer means of corrupting the sheep of Christ than by submitting them during their earlier years to anti-Christian and immoral systems of education. Hence the untiring efforts of the enemies of the Catholic faith everywhere to get the education of the people into their own hands or under their control. On the other hand, the Church, as in duty bound, has never ceased to meet this danger in such ways as lay within her means, both by providing suitable education for the young, and by condemning the false educational principles and systems of her adversaries, and warning the faithful against allowing themselves to get entangled in them. Now it cannot be said with any colour of justice that the Church, in passing judgment on systems of education, has exceeded her powers. For these systems are manifestly dogmatic and moral facts, owing to their necessary bearing upon dogma and morality. As such, then, the Church has a right to judge them; and since the faithful are bound to submit without appeal to her judgment upon these systems, she must be able to judge them infallibly. The Brief "Quum non" of Pius IX. to the Archbishop of Freiburg (1864) is a practical proof that the Church claims to speak authoritatively on the subject of education. Though the document, from its great importance, might well be quoted at full length, the following passages are especially noteworthy, both on account of their dogmatic character and the principles they lay down :—

"There is no doubt that most grievous injury must accrue to human society wherever the guiding authority of the Church is removed from the public and private education of youth.

"An education which forms the tender mind and easily perverted heart of youth without the aid of Christian doctrine and moral discipline cannot fail to produce an offspring which will be the cause of the greatest calamities both to private families and the State.

"While, however, this most pernicious system of teaching in separation from the Catholic faith and the Church's power is a source of the greatest hurt to individuals and society, when the question concerns giving instruction in letters and in the severer studies, and imparting education in public schools and institutions destined for the higher classes of society, nevertheless, who does not see that much more grievous harm will follow if this system be introduced into the schools of the common people?

"In these latter schools religious education ought to

occupy the first place, and everything else be regarded as accessories."

The Church would not speak thus dogmatically about education if the subject did not belong, though of course indirectly, to her teaching office.

(*h.*) *Particular Moral Facts.*

By these we mean facts which involve a principle of morality, and are its concrete expression. Such are the following:—A specified contract is usurious, and therefore a sin; it is unlawful to accept a challenge from fear of being thought a coward: as a rule, it is not lawful to kill a robber in order to preserve a gold piece. The Church can judge these facts infallibly, because of the moral principles they involve. If she did not decide such questions, she would be practically unable to check the spread of immoral doctrines among the faithful; and if she could not decide them infallibly she would be in danger of formally teaching immorality. Hence she has always regarded this power as implied in her commission as teacher, and she has never shrunk from condemning concrete moral propositions, under pain of excommunication to be incurred by those who taught or defended them, whenever she judged that these propositions were incompatible with purity of faith and morals.

4.—POLITICAL TRUTHS AND PRINCIPLES.

Leaving now the class of subjects comprised under the head of moral and dogmatic facts, we come to another branch of truth which the Church claims as belonging indirectly to the sphere of her teaching office. Politics, or the science which treats of the State, its rights, duties, and relations, presents from its ethical character many points of contact with revealed truth. The principles on which it is based flow from the natural law. They can never, therefore, be in real contradiction with the precepts of the Divine and positive law. Hence the State, if it only remain true to its fundamental principles, must ever be in the completest harmony with the Church and revelation. Now so long as this harmony continues, the Church has neither call nor right to interfere with the State, for earthly politics do not fall within her direct jurisdiction. The moment, however, the State becomes unfaithful to its principles, and contravenes the Divine and positive law, that moment it is the Church's right and duty, as guardian of revealed truth, to interfere, and to proclaim to the State the truths which it has ignored, and to condemn the erroneous maxims which it has adopted. Unhappily the State has too often given the Church occasion for interference, and false doctrines in politics have always found adherents, because they pandered to the greed of power and money, as well as to the abhorrence of control, which are so deeply rooted in our fallen nature. In former days, when civil society was leavened with the principles of the faith, the Church, by entering into direct communication with the rulers of different States, could often quietly impede the spread of error, and allay, by personal influence, the evil consequences arising from false principles of government. But what was possible then is not possible now, when society is unchristianizing itself more and more every day, and kings and statesmen habitually assume a position of open hostility or haughty distrust towards the Church. Therefore of late years she has been forced to lift up her voice, and from the Chair of Peter to cry aloud to the faithful throughout the world in accents of solemn warning against the pernicious errors with which the political atmosphere is everywhere loaded. It would take far too long to particularize these denunciations of false doctrine. The principal of them may be found in the Encyclical "Quanta Cura" (1864) of Pius IX., and the Syllabus of condemned propositions appended to it. No one can read through these documents without being convinced that the Church claims the right to distinguish error from truth in the domain of political science. And if she claims the right, according to the principles of the faith, she possesses it.

5.—Theological Conclusions.

We will now consider another class of truths which come under the Church's authority as teacher. They may be termed theological conclusions, using the word in its widest sense to express all propositions logically deducible from premises, one of which is revealed. The relation in which these propositions stand to revealed dogma, and therefore to the teaching office of the Church, will be better understood if we premise a few remarks upon the nature of theological science.

Faith, then, is a supernatural power infused into the soul, by which we are enabled to believe on God's authority with absolute certainty all the revealed truths which the Church proposes to us for belief. These truths, when once apprehended and accepted by faith, take their place in the believer's mind side by side with the other truths which he naturally possesses, or has acquired. Thus they add to, and form part of the sum total of his knowledge. Now, the human mind when cultivated has an instinctive tendency to reflect upon the truths which it possesses, to analyze them, to study their relations, to compare them with one another, to draw inferences from this comparison, to compare anew these inferences with other truths, and thus to go on continually enlarging its intellectual horizon. This is called to philosophize, and the result of the process is science. But revealed truth differs from natural truth only in the ground on which it rests in the believer's mind; namely, the authority of God. For, like natural truth, it must be clothed in words, and cast in the form of a proposition before it can be turned to account by the understanding, and it is only in this shape that it can be treasured up in the memory. Hence it enjoys no exceptional position in the mind, but is subject to precisely the same general laws as those which regulate the action of the intellect upon natural truth. Thus it is capable of being treated philosophically, and a science can be evolved from it. This science is theology.

The object-matter of this science, by which it is distinguished from all other special sciences, is God and the works of God as faith views them in the light of revelation. And its first principles, or fundamental premises, are truths of faith supplemented by truths whose evidence is purely natural.

The conclusions at which theology arrives are of two different kinds.

The first class is strictly scientific, since they are certainties. For science deals with certainties, and its results, if scientific, are certain. This class of theological conclusions is composed of inferences logically drawn from premises, one of which is a truth of faith, and the other a natural certainty, whether metaphysical, physical, or moral, using this last in the highest sense of the word. There can be no question that the Church is able to pronounce judgment upon conclusions of this class, since they stand in such direct connection with the faith. Not only can she judge them, but, according to the opinion of very many theologians, she can, if she pleases, define that they are virtually revealed, and propose them to the faithful for belief as of faith.

But besides these certain theological conclusions, there is another very extensive class about which we can have no absolute certainty. These are inferences from premises, one of which has been revealed or is deducible from revelation, while the other is only probably true, that is to say, valid but not conclusive reasons can be alleged in support of it. Of course, theological inferences of this class will differ very much from one another in their degree of probability. Some may be very dubious, while others approach the confines of moral certainty. But they must not be undervalued because they are not absolutely certain. For not only are they a natural and necessary result of theological speculation, but they fill an important office in regard to theology, since they help to place in a variety of lights and so to illustrate the abstruser dogmas of the faith. They are, in fact, a sort of outwork to revealed doctrine, the truth of which they imply and on which, in part, they rest. Hence, the Church watches over them with care, and fails not to condemn any conclusion of this kind which offends in form, expression, or substance against the revealed deposit. For though she may not always be able to judge concerning the absolute truth of such conclusions, she certainly can determine negatively that they are in contradiction, if so be, with the faith. Thus, we may infer from what has been said, that all theological conclusions, certain or probable, belong either positively or negatively to the object-matter of the Church's infallibility.

6.—Philosophy and Natural Sciences.

If we believe, as every Catholic must do, that whatever God hath revealed and proposed to our belief by the Church is absolutely true, it would be irrational in us to admit the barest possibility of a contradiction between any of the truths of faith and those for which reason vouches, whether on the ground of their intrinsic evidence, or because they have been correctly deduced from self-evident truths. The light of reason is God's gift no less than the light of faith; and since God cannot contradict Himself, what He reveals to faith must be in perfect harmony with all that reason manifests. If there is an apparent conflict between a revealed truth and a proposition deduced by reasoning from natural premises, either it is only apparent, or, if the two be really at variance and inconsistent with each other, it is evident that what is revealed must be true, and what has been inferred by reasoning must be erroneous. We may reason incorrectly, but we cannot be mistaken in regarding as infallible truth every dogma of the faith. We have, then, in the truths of revelation a touchstone by which error, hidden under the disguise of truth, can be infallibly detected. Whatever doctrine is inconsistent with the Catholic faith, however specious and well supported it may seem to be, is self-convicted of imposture. It cannot be true, because it contradicts that which is the most certain of all truth—the revelation of God, who can neither deceive nor be deceived.

Now to apply these principles. Philosophy and the natural sciences rest entirely on natural truths, out of which they are evolved and built up by processes of the reason. Thus far the Church has nothing to do with them. She neither supplies them with their principles nor superintends the mode of their evolution from these principles. But the case is different with regard to the conclusions at which science professes to have arrived. The Church cannot remain indifferent to them. For through the unskilfulness of the philosopher, or the use of an incorrect method of philosophizing, or the introduction of false premises, the results of what pretends to be scientific research may easily prove to be in opposition to the truths of faith. But when viewed in relation to the faith they cease to be purely secular in character. The Church, as teacher, receives thereby jurisdiction over them, and it becomes her right and duty, for her children's sake, to declare them, if so be, erroneous. She forms, however, this judgment concerning them, not by working over again the process which the philosopher had gone through, and thus discovering where his error lay, but by comparing his results with revealed truth, and estimating them accordingly. Thus, one who sees, corrects at a glance the faulty conclusions which a blind man has slowly and painfully arrived at, by touch and hearing, regarding the shape and position of certain objects. This he does, not by touch and hearing, but by another sense, sight, of which the blind man is destitute. In like manner the Church, whose eyes are opened to the light of faith, is able by the aid of this supernatural light to declare infallibly that a philosophical system or proposition or book is unsound, and she has many times in the course of her history exercised this power, when her children's needs required it. As an early example of such condemnations we may instance the decree of Clement V., issued with the approbation of the Œcumenical Council of Vienne (1311); by which the Pope "reprobates as erroneous and hostile to the truth of the Catholic faith every doctrine which rashly asserts or represents as dubious that the substance of the rational or intellectual soul is not truly and of itself the form of the body," and the decree goes on "to define that whoever, thenceforth shall presume to assert, defend, or hold that the rational or intellectual soul is not of itself and essentially the form of the human body, is to be regarded as a heretic." With regard to modern times, we need only refer to the proscription by the Apostolic See of the works of Hermes, Gunther, and Frohschammer, and for the censure of particular philosophical propositions to the Syllabus attached to the Encyclical "Quanta Cura." There can be no doubt about the power practically claimed by the Church over philosophy and science, and here we might fairly leave it, since what the Church claims she has a right to claim. But the subject is one of such importance, both in itself and in reference to questions of the day, that it will be well to quote in addition the words of Pius IX. in his dogmatic Brief "Inter Gravissimas"

(1862) to the Archbishop of Munich, in condemnation of certain writings of Frohschammer. They contain a luminous and authoritative exposition of the Church's relation to philosophy and science, and enforce her right to proscribe error in whatever department of human speculation she may come across it.

"There prevails in the above-mentioned works of this author another opinion, which is manifestly opposed to the doctrine and sentiment of the Catholic Church. For he attributes to philosophy a liberty which deserves to be called, not a liberty of science, but a philosophical licence, altogether worthy of reprobation, and intolerable. Distinguishing between the philosopher and philosophy, he asserts that it is the philosopher's right and duty to submit himself to the authority which has approved itself to him as true; but he in such sense denies this right and duty to philosophy as to assert that—taking no account of revealed doctrine—it never ought to, nor can, submit itself to authority. This statement might be tolerated, and perhaps even admitted, if it were merely meant to refer to the right which philosophy has of using its own principles or method, and its own conclusions, like other sciences, and if the liberty attributed to it consisted only in using this its right in such sort as to refuse to admit into itself anything which it had not acquired in its own way, or which was foreign to it. But this rightful liberty of philosophy ought to know its own limits and to keep within them. For it will never be lawful either for the philosopher or for philosophy to say aught contrary to the things taught by divine revelation and the Church, nor to throw a doubt upon any of these things because of not understanding them, nor to decline to accept a judgment pronounced by the Church's authority upon a philosophical conclusion which till then was open. Moreover, the same writer maintains the liberty, or rather the unrestrained licence of philosophy, so vehemently and rashly, that he hesitates not to assert that the Church not only never ought to proceed vigorously against, but ought even to tolerate the errors of, philosophy, and to leave it to correct itself: from which it follows that philosophers necessarily share in this liberty of philosophy, and thus themselves also are set free from every law. Who does not see how energetically this opinion and doctrine of Frohschammer ought to be rejected, reprobated, and utterly condemned? For the Church, in virtue of her divine institution, is bound both to keep most diligently whole and inviolate the deposit of divine faith, and to watch unceasingly with all earnestness over the salvation of souls; as also most carefully to remove and eliminate all those things which may be opposed to the faith or in any way endanger the salvation of souls. Wherefore the Church, in virtue of the power entrusted to her by her divine Author, has the right and obligation not only of refusing to tolerate, but also of proscribing and condemning all errors, if the integrity of the faith and the salvation of souls demand it; and all philosophers who wish to be sons of the Church, and philosophy itself likewise, are bound in duty never to say anything contrary to the Church's teaching, and to retract those things about which she may have admonished them. Moreover, We decree and declare that the opinion which teaches the contrary to this is altogether erroneous and in the highest degree insulting to the faith of the Church and her authority."

These words of the Sovereign Pontiff need no comment. They will go home of themselves to the heart and understanding of every Catholic.

And now, looking back at the ground which we have traversed, we may thus gather up the results of our investigation into the object-matter of the Church's infallibility. We began by placing before us the Church as our teacher, and we contemplated her, not under the form of a vague abstraction, but as a living personality, possessed of an intellect with which to judge and a voice with which to speak, dwelt in by the Spirit of truth, and infallible in all her judgments and pronouncements. Moreover, we saw that she was intrusted by our Lord with the deposit of the faith and commissioned to instruct all nations in it, and to keep His flock pure from all doctrine contrary to the faith and to their eternal well-being. But no revealed truth, we remarked, can be in contradiction with any natural truth. If such seems to be the case, either the contradiction is only apparent, or else that which we fancy to be a natural truth is self-convicted of being an error. Hence the Church can judge the results of human science by applying to them the standard of the faith, of which she is the guardian, and if she finds that they are at variance with the faith, she has the right to condemn them as erroneous; and since this right flows indirectly from her office as infallible teacher of the faith, her condemnation of them must be infallible. Again, we perceived that truth, whether supernatural or natural, is often found embodied in concrete facts, in which fact and truth are so united that the truth cannot be judged unless the fact be indirectly judged along with it. And we thence inferred that the Church must have power to estimate infallibly the value of such facts, be they dogmatic, moral, or political; else, if she could not discriminate with certainty between embodiments of truth and embodiments of error, she would be wanting in what is strictly necessary for the due fulfilment of her office as teacher of the universal flock.

Thus, then, to combine these detached results into one general view, we may say that the object-matter of the Church's infallibility embraces primarily and directly all revealed truth, whether explicitly or implicitly contained in the revealed deposit; and secondarily and indirectly all natural truths, both of fact and speculation, which stand in such relation to revealed truth that error concerning them would tend to impair the integrity of the faith in the minds of Christians and to imperil their eternal salvation.

IV.

We have now reached, in the course of this inquiry, the fourth question which we proposed at starting to investigate; the way, namely, in which the Church exercises her office as teacher. This clearly must in great measure depend on the kind and amount of work which she is called upon, as teacher, to perform. We will therefore begin by trying to ascertain what she teaches, and afterwards pass on to consider how she teaches it.

The Catholic Church, then,—to use the word in its

widest sense as the assemblage of the faithful in communion with the Apostolic See,—is a body politic, organized as a kingdom, extending throughout the whole world, and embracing within its circuit men of every variety of race, nationality, class, and condition. This is its earthly aspect. And from this point of view, as a visible society of men under a visible monarch with a complete external organization and unity, it presents a close resemblance to the kingdoms of this world, while at the same time it differs from them essentially in the supernaturalness of its origin, end, and constitution. But whence comes it that the elements of which the Church is composed, though naturally so heterogeneous and conflicting, coalesce into one compact and permanent body? What is the reason that cruel and long-continued persecutions have been powerless to break it up? How has it been able to withstand the dissolving influence which the attractions of other centres—political, national, or intellectual—are unceasingly exercising upon its members? In a word, what is the cause of the Church's unity? To answer this, we must remember that the Church, in so far as it is a visible body politic, must conform itself to the general laws which govern all political associations and are the conditions of their existence. For the supernatural order does not destroy the natural, but builds upon and perfects it, while it lifts men to a state high above the highest which is attainable by any powers inherent in or due to nature. Hence innumerable analogies may be traced between these two orders, and nature is ever foreshadowing what grace exhibits with a supernatural completeness. Let us then inquire whence comes the unity of an earthly kingdom. This will help us better to understand how it is that the kingdom of heaven upon earth, as our Lord again and again termed His Church, is most intimately one.

The primary and adequate cause of an earthly kingdom's unity is the supreme authority of the sovereign who rules over it, and to whom all acknowledge that they owe obedience. This is alone sufficient to bind into one body provinces and states which differ from each other fundamentally in religion, history, interests, and affections. Still it must be admitted that a kingdom, or an aggregate of kingdoms, which has no other principle of unity than this external bond, may indeed be called an united kingdom or an empire, but is not one body in the fullest meaning of the word. Who, for instance, would say that England, Ireland, and India are one in the same sense that England south of the Tweed is one? The several portions which compose it possess, though latently, all that is necessary for separate existence, and if by treaty, conquest, or otherwise, the tie is broken, they easily reorganize themselves round fresh centres of authority, and the desire for reunion is scarcely felt or soon disappears. But it is possible for a kingdom to be one in a far more perfect way. Its members may be knit together, not only by the bond of subjection to a common sovereign, but they may be one internally. This will be the case when they have a common treasure of thoughts, sympathies, aims, interests, and memories, peculiar to themselves and incommunicable to others, inherited from those who went before, to be transmitted to those who will come after, and giving a similar tinge and bend to the whole moral and intellectual being of all who share in it. Such states form one homogeneous whole, and their members are bound together by an interior and indestructible attraction, so that the separation of any part from the rest is like tearing away a limb from a living body. The dynasties which rule them may change; the form of government may vary; the wave of conquest may pass over them; but they still remain after every change or disaster one people, and, if divided externally by superior force, they yearn and strive after reunion.

The Catholic Church is a kingdom of this second kind. It is one exteriorly in virtue of the obedience every Catholic pays to the Sovereign Pontiff. And it is one interiorly, because all its members are knit together in the belief and profession of the one faith. We have already considered the exterior bond of the Church's unity, namely, the plenitude of power bestowed by Christ upon His Vicar. We have now to examine that which makes the Church one interiorly; and it is a question which deserves our best attention, for certainly a power which can thus bind the Church together, and constitute a unity which eighteen centuries have been unable to dissolve, must in the nature of things be a mighty power. The Catholic faith can be no mere bundle of indefinite propositions, lying dormant and isolated in the believer's mind. It may, indeed, be cast into the shape of propositions, and it can only be communicated to others, or reflected upon by its possessor under this form. But they are propositions which represent truths of the highest order and the most momentous interest, and which take their place as absolute certainties in the minds of the faithful. They are pregnant with innumerable consequences, fertile in the variety of their application, and related in manifold ways to every branch of human speculation and action. He who possesses these truths is raised thereby to a higher intellectual level than the rest of men. He sees all things from a truer point of view, and estimates them by correcter standards. He has an interior life of belief, affection, aim, and hope, to which they are strangers. And in the possession of this life he finds himself already one with all who share it with him, a member with them of a heavenly commonwealth, which has indeed necessarily a visible form and organization, and is bound together exteriorly by the indispensable tie of obedience to its common head, but the ground and foundation of whose oneness lies within.

We see now the nature of the work which the Church as teacher has to perform. It consists in communicating to her children, one by one, generation after generation, that body of supernatural truth which is the interior condition of their corporate life. And this she has to do in such a manner as will most effectually steep their hearts and minds in the faith, and saturate their whole intellectual being with its principles. At the same time, she has to be ever on the watch that they do not diverge one hair's breadth from the faith, or adopt opinions even remotely inconsistent with its integrity. This must be a difficult task, even from a natural point of view; but how much harder does it appear when we call to mind that the habit of faith is a supernatural gift which needs to be sedulously guarded, since unbelief or doubt will forfeit it, and that the truths of faith are also supernatural, and may therefore easily become corrupted and perish, unless the teacher is ever at hand to inculcate them anew, and to deepen and refresh the impression of them.

Such is the work which the Church, as teacher, has to do. What, then, are the means she uses to accomplish it? This is what we have now to investigate.

The ordinary and regular mode by which the Church labours to imbue her children with the faith consists principally in a direct and personal action exerted upon them one by one. To effect this, she possesses in her clergy a numerous and organized band of teachers, through whom she is able to reach and come into contact with each individual member of her flock, and thus to learn and supply the spiritual wants of each. By this means none of her children are left without a pastor whose duty it is to know his sheep personally, to watch over their well-being, and to feed them individually with the pasture of Catholic doctrine. In every parish the Church has established schools for the young, and she fails not to superintend with unceasing care the teaching which is imparted in them. She provides for the ordinary education of her clergy seminaries specially destined for that object, and while she has always encouraged her children to a deeper and more scientific pursuit of truth in the universities of which she was the foundress or the foster-mother, she has never ceased to superintend with jealous eye the studies pursued in them, and to banish from them every doctrine and method which was not in perfect harmony with revealed truth. But besides this direct action which the Church exercises upon the flock, her ritual and liturgy, the fasts and festivals as they recur, processions, images, shrines, special devotions public and private, the disciplinary laws which regulate her organization, her monastic and charitable institutions—these and a multitude of other things of like nature, conduce powerfully though indirectly to the same end, since they serve to bring home to the faithful, and so to teach them the truths of faith which they embody, and on which they rest. They are, in fact, a kind of incarnation of the faith, and when interpreted by the voice of the living teacher produce a most powerful and abiding impression on those who live within their influence. This method of imparting the faith to Christians, partly direct and partly indirect, is what is called, in technical language, the Church's ordinary magisterium.

But, it may be asked, what security have we that this vast body of teachers, none of whom are personally infallible, will transmit the faith to their disciples in its original purity, and not teach falsehood instead of truth? How does the Church's infallibility come in here to guarantee their teaching from all error? The security we seek lies in the position of entire dependence which the inferior clergy occupy towards the bishops in whose dioceses they live and teach. It is from his bishop that each one of them receives his mission to teach, according to the Apostle's words, "How shall they preach unless they are sent?" (Rom. x. 15). It is under his bishop's eye that he teaches; and it is to his bishop that he is responsible for all he teaches. No supervision can be imagined more effective and no subordination more complete. Thus the bishops are the guarantees of the orthodoxy of their clergy's teaching. And with regard to the bishops themselves, we have a double security. First, in the principles of hierarchical subordination; for, as the clergy depend on the bishop, so the bishop depends on the Pope; and as it is the bishop's right and duty to silence any of his clergy whose teaching is unsound, so it is the Pope's right and duty to impose silence upon a heretical bishop, and to take from him the portion of the flock which had been intrusted to him. Secondly, in the certainty which the promised assistance of the Holy Ghost gives us, that the Ecclesia Docens—*i.e.*, the whole Episcopate in union with the Pope, cannot err in the faith, nor suffer even a temporary suspension of its teaching functions. What more effectual guarantee can be desired for the practical infallibility of the body of teachers through whose agency the Church imbues her children with the faith?

Having said thus much about the manner in which the Church communicates the faith to her flock, we may pass on to examine the means she employs to guard her sheep against the invasion and corrupting influence of erroneous doctrines. For heresies have abounded from the very times of the Apostles, and will continue to abound until the end.

The first and ordinary way in which the Church seeks to expel pernicious doctrine from the fold, is by impressing more earnestly than usual upon her children in her everyday teaching the doctrines of the faith which have been specially impugned. And the deeper the faith is rooted in their hearts, and the more completely they are possessed and animated by its principles, the more easy is it for the Church thus to nip error in the bud, and to cast forth the poison before it has had time to do much injury to the flock. It was in this way that during the first three centuries of the Christian Æra, when persecution was incessantly winnowing out from among the faithful all half-hearted members, many heresies were withered up, and brought to an untimely end. And so, too, in the Middle Ages, when the whole framework of society was moulded upon the faith, and in every department of speculation the truths of faith were regarded as absolute certainties to which all else must bend, erroneous doctrines were sometimes held in check for a long time, if not finally eradicated, by the mere force of the Church's daily teaching and personal influence.

But cases would occur from time to time, and must necessarily occur, which demanded stronger remedies and another method of procedure. Heresies arose so subtle in character, and so cunningly disguised under the garb of tolerated doctrine, as to perplex and divide for a time even the learned. Again, opinions out of harmony with the Church's teaching on subjects only distantly related to the faith, would gain ground for a time in particular portions of the fold. And since the opposition of these opinions to the faith was not evident at first sight, discussion and dispute would follow, calling for an authoritative decision to allay them. Or, again, a heresy would spread like a pestilence among the flock, and carry off thousands and tens of thousands from the faith. In these and similar cases the Church's ordinary mode of teaching would be inadequate to meet the evil. She must raise her voice and speak aloud to the whole body of the faithful, and by a solemn and official pronouncement draw the line sharply between truth and falsehood, and thus secure her children from the danger of unwitting error, and leave the rebels without excuse.

Such a pronouncement on a disputed point of doctrine cannot be had without a tribunal to sift and judge the question ; and if the pronouncement is to be infallible and irreformable, the tribunal must be an infallible one. Now the Church, as we have already seen, possesses, in the Sovereign Pontiff alone and in the Episcopate united to the Sovereign Pontiff, a twofold tribunal of this character. Its more imposing and solemn form is that of an Œcumenical Council, when the bishops of the Universal Church, summoned and presided over by the Vicar of Christ their head, sit in judgment upon error, and declare to the flock what is obligatory upon their belief. Thus it was that the subtle and wide-spread heresy of Arius was condemned at Nice (325), and the no less impious tenets of Luther and his fellow-reformers at Trent (1545—1563). And so again the Council of the Vatican has been convoked (1869) by Pius IX. to proscribe the errors which are most prevalent in the present day, and are therefore most full of danger to the faithful. The Councils of Nice and of the Vatican are the first and last Œcumenical Councils which have been held, and, in the interval of fifteen centuries which lies between them, there have been only seventeen other Œcumenical Councils. It was not that the heresies and errors which sprang up during this period were few and unimportant, but an Œcumenical Council is an extraordinary tribunal, which from its nature the Church can only employ occasionally, and under peculiar circumstances. The ordinary and standing form of her infallible tribunal is the Sovereign Pontiff alone, and this is abundantly sufficient for all the common requirements of the faithful; the convocation of an Œcumenical Council being rather a matter of expedience than of necessity. The Vicar of Christ is always within reach, and appeal can be made to him without difficulty from the most distant part of the fold. Moreover, placed as he is on the watch-tower of Israel, with his eyes unintermittingly directed to every part of the universal flock, the needs and dangers of no portion of it can escape his vigilance, and he has the means of judging, as no one else has, how and when to crush false and dangerous doctrines by his infallible pronouncements. Accordingly, we find that while Œcumenical Councils have been rare events in the Church's history, the Sovereign Pontiff from the Chair of Peter has never ceased to lift up his warning voice, age after age, in condemnation of the errors which were threatening the flock, and to proclaim anew the truths which the world was in danger of forgetting.

The Pope, as we have just seen, has the power to teach infallibly; and he exercises this power from time to time, as the needs of the Church require it. But it must not be supposed that he is at all times and on all occasions raised above the possibility of error. He is liable to make mistakes as other people in his private capacity; for example, in conversation, or in preaching, or in writing books, even on theology. He may err, too, as Head of the Church when deciding a question of fact relating to persons, or giving advice to individuals who may have consulted him. His infallibility attaches only to the official acts which, in his character of universal teacher, he addresses to the whole Church, requiring at the same time from all the faithful absolute interior assent. It is of little consequence how he manifests his intention of exacting intellectual submission, whether by the threat of anathema upon the disobedient, or by the mere use of language implying a grave precept. That he commands our assent is a sufficient sign that what he bids us believe is true.

From what has been said, it is plain that the simple omission to define a dogma or to condemn an error, even though the neglect were culpable and hurtful to the Church, is in no way inconsistent with the prerogative of infallibility. For the Pope is infallible only when he teaches; and to teach is one thing, and to omit to teach another. Again, if the Pope is not a free agent, his teaching is not infallible: hence decrees made by him under the constraint of tortures, imprisonment, or grievous menaces, would not necessarily be free from error. Moreover, his infallibility does not extend beyond the subject-matter of the Church's infallibility, and is therefore limited to revealed truth and whatever bears upon it. Even in the case of an infallible decree it is only the doctrine ruled, and not the grounds alleged in support of the ruling, which is exempt from the possibility of error. With respect to those things which usually precede dogmatic pronouncements—such as prayer, invocation of the Holy Ghost, investigations, consultations, and the like,—it is certain that they are in no sense necessary to the infallibility of the subsequent decree. Doubtless there is a propriety in the use of these preliminaries, since infallibility is not, like prophecy, an interior illumination descending upon the soul from above, but consists merely in an external guarantee against an erroneous pronouncement. Still, the promise of infallibility is to the Pope alone, and not to his counsellors or investigations; and it belongs to God's providence in ordaining the end to secure the use of the means requisite for attaining the end. Besides, if it were once admitted that the infallibility of the decree depends upon the preparatory acts, heretics would always object that the question determined had not been sufficiently examined, and on this plea refuse obedience to the Pope's teaching. Hence, when once the Pope has spoken and commanded submission, no Catholic may venture for an instant to suspend his assent. The mere fact that he has spoken is proof enough that he has grounds for what he says.

The special form which the Sovereign Pontiffs may choose to adopt when they teach the Universal Church is, from the nature of the case, a matter of indifference so long as they address all the faithful, and require submission of the intellect to their decrees. It may be by Bull, or Brief, or Encyclical, or in a Consistorial Allocution. All these forms have been and are still used. Again, they may direct their decree to the Universal Church in express terms, or they may do so equivalently by writing to a particular church or even to an individual, provided always they take measures to insure the subsequent promulgation of their decree to all the faithful. The well-known dogmatic letter of S. Leo I. to S. Flavian is an instance in point. They may also extract propositions from documents which they had previously addressed to particular bishops or even to laymen, and by a new act of promulgation make these propositions obligatory upon the assent of every Christian. An example of this is furnished by the syllabus of errors put forth by Pius IX. in 1864.

Encyclicals or circular letters, directed to all bishops in communion with the Holy See, have often been employed, especially of late years, by the Sovereign Pontiffs as a convenient mode of teaching the faithful. It was in this manner that the philosophical errors of La Mennais were condemned by Gregory XVI. in the celebrated Encyclical "Mirari vos" (1832), to which he required internal assent as well as exterior submission. Again, the same Sovereign Pontiff, Gregory XVI., in the brief by which he condemned the works of Hermes (1835), after speaking of the dangerous errors which were being propagated under the disguise of philosophy, goes on to say:—

"Wherefore, as soon as the impious and insidious attempts of certain of these writers became known to Us, *We did not delay by Our Encyclical and other Apostolic Letters* to denounce their cunning and evil counsels, and *to condemn their errors*, and at the same time to make manifest the deadly deceptions with which they most artfully endeavour to overthrow from the foundations the divine constitution of the Church and ecclesiastical discipline; nay, even the whole public order of things."

He then proscribes the books of Hermes as full of unsound doctrine, and concludes with an exhortation to all bishops and ordinaries:—

"That, being mindful of the strict and most severe judgment which awaits them from the Prince of pastors, with regard to their rule and watchfulness over the flock committed to them, they not only expel the aforesaid books from the schools, but also strive with all care and solicitude to turn away their own sheep from such poisoned pastures."

Still more memorable is the Encyclical "Quanta cura," issued by Pius IX. in 1864. We will quote from it several passages which illustrate very forcibly what we have said, and exemplify the way in which the Sovereign Pontiffs are accustomed to teach the Church.

At the very beginning of this letter the Pope, as if to show that it was in his capacity of pastor and teacher of the Universal Church that he was writing, makes a pointed allusion to the office of feeding the flock of Christ, which belongs in an especial manner to the successors of St. Peter :—

" With how great care and vigilance the Roman Pontiffs, Our predecessors, fulfilling the duty and office committed to them by the Lord Christ Himself in the person of the most Blessed Peter, Prince of the Apostles, of feeding the lambs and the sheep, have never ceased sedulously to *nourish the Lord's whole flock with words of faith and with salutary doctrine, and to guard it from poisoned pastures*, is thoroughly known to all, and especially to you, Venerable Brethren."

After this introduction the Pope continues :—" And in truth, these our predecessors, deeply solicitous for the salvation of souls, had nothing more at heart than by their most wise *Letters and Constitutions to unveil and condemn all those heresies and errors which, being adverse to our Divine Faith, to the Catholic Church, to purity of morals, and to the eternal salvation of men* . . . have afflicted both Church and State." Then adverting to what he himself had done, he adds :—" It is well known to you, Venerable Brethren, that no sooner were We, by the secret counsel of Divine Providence, and through no merits of Our own, raised to this Chair of Peter, than, following the example of Our predecessors, We raised Our voice, and *in many published Encyclical Letters and Allocutions delivered in Consistory, and other Apostolic Letters, We condemned the chief errors* of this Our unhappy age.

" And especially in *Our first Encyclical Letter*, written to you Nov. 9, 1846, and in *two Allocutions* delivered by Us in Consistory, the one on Dec. 9, 1854, and the other on June 9, 1862, *We condemned the monstrous portents of opinion* which prevail in this age, bringing with them the greatest loss of souls, and detriment of civil society itself; which are grievously opposed also not only to the Catholic Church and her salutary doctrine and venerable rights, but also to the eternal natural law engraven by God in all men's hearts and to right reason, and from which almost all other errors have their origin."

The Pope then goes on to enumerate and condemn various doctrines and propositions ; after which, towards the close of the letter, he speaks as follows :—

" Amidst, therefore, such great perversity of depraved opinions, We, *well remembering Our Apostolic office*, and very greatly solicitous for Our most holy religion, for sound doctrine, and the salvation of the souls entrusted to Us, and for the welfare of human society itself, *have thought it right again to raise Our Apostolic voice. Therefore by Our Apostolic authority We reprobate, proscribe, and condemn all and singular the evil opinions and doctrines severally mentioned in this letter, and will and command that they be thoroughly held by all children of the Catholic Church as reprobated, proscribed, and condemned."*

Now surely an Encyclical containing passages like these, which are even stronger in their context than as extracts, has every mark about it of an *ex cathedrâ* or infallible pronouncement. For either it was not the Pope's intention in this letter to teach the universal flock from the chair of Peter, and to bind all the faithful to an interior submission to his decrees,—but in this case he could not have used words more calculated to perplex and lead us astray,—or he did intend to oblige us to assent under pain of sin; and if so, he is infallible in what he has defined. This is the dilemma in which we find ourselves. To decide between these alternatives, we have only to reflect upon the last-quoted passage from the Encyclical, and then ask ourselves whether it is possible for us, as Catholics, with good conscience, to regard as tenable any one of " the evil opinions and doctrines " therein " reprobated, proscribed, and condemned," and which the Vicar of Christ "wills and commands" shall "be thoroughly held by all children of the Catholic Church as reprobated, proscribed, and condemned."

But if this Encyclical is an infallible pronouncement, we have the Pope's warrant for saying that a similar character and authority belong to such other of his Encyclicals, Consistorial Allocutions, and Apostolic Letters as are condemnatory of false doctrine. For it would be unreasonable to suppose that the Sovereign Pontiff had intended by means of them " solemnly to condemn the chief errors of this most unhappy age," without having meant at the same time to bind the faithful to assent interiorly to the condemnation. A like character of infallibility belongs to the Syllabus of condemned propositions, which was promulgated and sent round to all the bishops of the Church by the command of the Holy Father. They, with one consent and the most unreserved submission, accepted it as the voice of Peter and the oracles of God. Certainly no Catholic can venture to reject the testimony of the whole Episcopate united to its Head.

And now to sum up in a few words the results of our inquiry into the way in which the Church exercises her office of teacher. Her ordinary method consists in an unwearied, every-day, personal inculcation of the truths of faith upon her individual members by means of her numerous clergy; coupled with the silent and indirect influence of her ritual, discipline, and institutions. But as this ordinary method is insufficient to meet all the cases which may arise, she has recourse, extraordinarily and occasionally, to another mode of promulgating the truth. This is by solemn and formal judgments in which she addresses the universal flock by the organ of an Œcumenical Council or of the Sovereign Pontiff, and either propounds some dogma of the faith, or brands erroneous doctrine with the censure which is appropriate to it. The form in which this is done is immaterial, provided always it expresses that a grave obligation is laid upon the faithful to assent interiorly to what is decreed.

V.

We may now proceed to the fifth point of our inquiry:—What are the nature and character of the Church's doctrinal condemnations? In answer to this question, we begin by observing that every condemnation, whatever may be its object, necessarily implies two things: first, a standard or measure by which the thing condemned is tested; and secondly, a judgment declaring that the thing is not in conformity with this standard. What, then, is the Church's standard by which she tests and condemns faulty doctrines? It can only be the deposit of the faith, including in this, of course, the general principles of the moral law. For she has no other standard by which to judge but this: and it is only from the point of view in which a given doctrine has a bearing upon revealed truth, and is therefore commensurable with it, that she regards it as subject to her jurisdiction. The Church's doctrinal condemnations are therefore equivalent to formal pronouncements that the particular doctrines she condemns are at variance in some point or other with the Catholic faith.

But, while all condemned doctrines agree in this, that they diverge from the standard of the faith, they differ very much from one another in the kind and degree of this divergence. The various modes in which they may stand opposed to the faith have been carefully examined by theologians, and expressed by a more or less fixed terminology; and a proposition is said to have been "censured," when sentence has been pronounced upon it indicating that it is out of harmony with the faith.

It is unnecessary to explain at length the many different ways in which faulty doctrines deflect from the revealed standard. We will merely give one or two instances as an illustration. Thus, a proposition may be directly opposed to some truth which is without question a dogma of faith. This would be qualified as "heretical." Again, without being directly opposed to revealed truth, it might contradict a theological conclusion, logically inferrible from premises both of which are certain, and one at least revealed. Such a proposition would be termed "erroneous." Again, though capable of a good and Catholic interpretation, the bad and heretical sense might be the more common and obvious one. This would deserve the note of "evil sounding." Again, it might be of such a character as would jar upon the ears of a pious person, that is, one devoted to the doctrine of the faith. It would in that case be noted as "offensive to pious ears." Or, lastly, it might be a proposition resting on no solid grounds, either intrinsic or extrinsic; or else it might be contrary to the general teaching of theologians. If so, it would be condemned as "temerarious." Such are a few of the ways in which faulty doctrine may diverge from the standard of the faith.

Now the Church, in the exercise of her office as teacher, claims the power not only of declaring infallibly that a given doctrine is in opposition to the revealed deposit, but of determining, if she pleases, the exact degree and kind of this opposition. In other words, she asserts her right to assign properly to each proposition which she condemns the censure which belongs to it. The particular way, however, in which she has exercised this power has varied at different periods of her history. For many centuries she was content to condemn unsound doctrines, either as heretical, or without affixing to them any special note. It was not until the fourteenth century that she began to qualify them with a distinct censure lower than "heretical." Thus, Clement V., with the approval of the Œcumenical Council of Vienne (1311), condemned a certain philosophical doctrine concerning the relation which exists between the human soul and body as "erroneous and hostile to the truth of the Catholic faith." And a few years later, John XXII. (1329), after enumerating twenty-eight propositions extracted from the writings of Eckard, pronounced that seventeen of these, which he specified, were "heretical," and the rest "evil sounding, temerarious, and suspected of heresy." Since then the practice of branding propositions and doctrines with censures inferior to "heretical," has become a matter of ordinary occurrence. There are three modes of doing this. Sometimes, as in the case of Eckard, each proposition is noted with the precise censure which it has incurred. It was in this way that Pius VI., by the Constitution "Auctorem fidei" (1794), censured eighty-five propositions taken from the decrees of the Synod of Pistoia. At other times a number of propositions are condemned in a body with the declaration that they deserve respectively certain specific censures. It was thus that the errors of Huss and Wickliff were proscribed by Martin V. and the Council of Constance, and those of Molinos and Quesnel by the Apostolic See. So also twenty-three propositions relating to the love of God were condemned by Innocent XII. in the brief "Cum alias" (1699), "as being, either in the obvious sense of the words, or with reference to the context, temerarious, scandalous, evil sounding, offensive to pious ears, pernicious in practice, and also respectively erroneous." We may observe that, when propositions are thus condemned *in globo*, every one of the propositions without exception is condemned; there is not one among them to which one at least of the censures enumerated is not applicable; and not a single censure is superfluous, but is merited by one at least of the propositions. Sometimes, again, a book is proscribed and prohibited without any propositions being extracted from it for special censure. Thus Pius VI., by the brief "Super soliditate" (1786), condemned the book "Quis est Papa?" as "containing propositions respectively false, scandalous, temerarious, injurious, leading to schism, schismatical, erroneous, leading to heresy, heretical, and otherwise condemned by the Church." But while the brief indicates the drift of the book, and the kind of errors it contains, no special propositions are extracted from it for reprobation.

In these three ways the Church has been accustomed, for the last five centuries, to condemn books and doctrines at variance with the faith. The selection of one mode rather than another in any particular case belongs entirely to ecclesiastical usage and prudence.

If at any time the Church does not think it expedient to affix to each separate proposition the censure which it individually merits, this is not from want of power, for she has done it again and again in other cases, but simply because the good of the flock, which is her primary aim, has been sufficiently secured by a more general mode of condemnation. It is enough for the faithful to be informed that certain propositions or books are unsound and should be avoided, even though they are not authoritatively informed what is the precise kind and degree of their unsoundness.

VI.

The sixth and last question which it remains for us to examine is the obligation which the Church's teaching lays upon the faithful.

The duty of obedience to the Church is one of the first principles of the Christian faith. No words can be more solemn and express than those in which our Blessed Lord imposed it on us. "If he will not hear the Church, let him be to thee as the heathen and the publican" (Matt. xviii. 17); and again, "He that heareth you heareth Me, and he that despiseth you despiseth Me" (Luke x. 16). Hence the Church comes to us as a teacher sent from God: "As My Father hath sent Me, I also send you" (John xx. 21); and with authority from God to teach, "Going therefore, teach ye all nations" (Matt. xxviii. 19); and with a threat of punishment against those who refuse to hear her teaching, "Whosoever shall not receive you, nor hear your words, amen, I say to you, it shall be more tolerable for the land of Sodom and Gomorrha in the day of judgment than for that city" (Matt. x. 14, 15). Now, as we did not choose the Church for our teacher, nor give her authority to teach us, so neither can we set limits to her teaching nor free ourselves from the obligation of obeying her. Her power comes from Christ, whom she represents. And since He has put no restriction on the obedience which she can claim from us, it follows that whatever she bids us do, we are bound to do, and whatever she bids us believe, we are bound to believe. Our obedience to her must be absolute, unbounded, and unreasoning, as to the voice of God Himself.

No Catholic would think of questioning the truth of this, at least as an abstract proposition. None, therefore, can deny, what is only its necessary consequence, that the nature of the obligation which the Church's teaching lays upon the faithful must depend entirely upon her own will in imposing it. She can bind us to what she pleases, and in what way she pleases. All, then, that we have to do is to ascertain what her intention is, and, when we have discovered it, we shall know the obligation which, as our teacher, she has laid upon us.

The Church's doctrinal decrees themselves will furnish us with the best and clearest evidence of her intention. They may be divided into two classes, in reference to the kind of submission which they impose upon us. The first class consists of those which require from the faithful nothing more than a certain external line of conduct regarding a particular doctrine, leaving the doctrine itself untouched by the decree. Thus, for example, after many disputations concerning the nature of efficacious grace had been held in the presence of successive Sovereign Pontiffs, between the representatives of opposing schools of Catholic theology, Clement XII., in a decree (1733) confirming various ordinances of his predecessors, forbade "that any one should dare to brand with a theological censure any of these schools, or assail their opinions with insult, until the Holy See should think fit to make a definition or pronouncement respecting these controversies." So again, to give another instance from the history of a doctrine which has recently been declared to be a dogma of the faith, Gregory XV., by the organ of the holy Roman Inquisition, published on 24th May, 1622, an edict, in which, after reciting and confirming the decree of Paul V., relative to the doctrine of the Immaculate Conception, he enacted that, "until the question was decided by the Apostolic See, or it was otherwise provided by the Holy See and his Holiness, no one should presume to assert, even in private conversation or writing, that the Blessed Virgin had been conceived with original sin, or to affirm in any way this opinion." Nevertheless, to show that this edict had reference only to discipline, and had no direct bearing upon doctrine, the Pope added that "His Holiness does not thereby intend to reprobate this opinion nor to do it any prejudice, but he leaves it in the same state and terms in which it now is, save only as regards the dispositions of the aforenamed decree of Paul V. and his own."

The prohibitory decrees are few in number, and from their nature demand only exterior submission from the faithful. But it is otherwise with the other and far more numerous class of doctrinal enactments. In them the Church pronounces a solemn judgment upon the deviation of certain doctrines from the standard of revealed truth; and requires from us interior assent to her decision. This deviation may amount to a formal contradiction of some proposition which is of faith, or it may be less than this. In the former case the doctrine merits the censure "heretical," and in the latter some lesser censure. No one doubts that every Catholic is bound to hold as heretical whatever the Church pronounces to be such; but are we also bound to believe that the minor censures affixed by the Church to particular doctrines are infallibly deserved by them? To answer this we have only to look at the recorded practice of the Church. If she requires us to accept with interior submission her decisions when she affixes any of the minor censures, it must be because she claims to be infallible in affixing them; and since what she claims, she has the right to claim, from her practice we may legitimately infer her infallibility.

The following instances will exhibit very clearly the kind of assent which she exacts from us, when she condemns doctrines with a lesser censure than that of heresy.

Martin V., in the Bull "Inter cunctas" (1418), by which he confirmed the decrees of the Council of Constance, after enumerating the particular errors of Wickliff and Huss, which the Council had singled out for condemnation, enjoins that if an "educated man" is suspected of entertaining these errors, he is "to be specially interrogated whether he *believes* that the sentence passed by the Sacred Council of Constance upon the forty-five articles of John Wickliff and the thirty articles of John Huss, given above, is true and Catholic: namely, that the aforesaid forty-five articles of John Wickliff and the thirty articles of John Huss are not Catholic, but *that some of them are notoriously heretical, some erroneous, some temerarious and seditious, and some offensive to pious ears.*"

Again, the Council of Constance in its last session (1418) prescribed a formula, according to which persons suspected of holding the errors of Wickliff and Huss were to be interrogated. Among the questions to be put to them occur the following :—

"Whether they *believe* that the condemnations of John Wickliff, John Huss, and Jerome of Prague, relative to their persons, books, and teaching, by the Sacred Council of Constance, were duly and justly passed, and ought to be held and firmly asserted as such by every Catholic. Also whether they *believe, hold*, and assert that John Wickliff, John Huss, and Jerome of Prague were heretics, and ought to be called and esteemed as heretics, and that their books and doctrines were and are perverse, on account of which books and doctrines, and their obstinacy, they were condemned by the Sacred Council of Constance."

Once more, Innocent XI., in the Constitution "Cœlestis Pastor" (1687), condemned sixty-eight propositions of Michael de Molinos, in the following terms :—

"We have condemned and branded these propositions as respectively heretical, suspicious, erroneous, scandalous, blasphemous, offensive to pious ears, temerarious, tending to relax and subvert Christian discipline, and seditious; and we have interdicted all persons in future from speaking, writing, and disputing about them, and from *believing, holding*, teaching, or practising them."

So, again, Clement XI., in the Bull "Unigenitus" (1713), after branding with no fewer than twenty-six different censures one hundred and one propositions taken from Quesnel's Commentary on the New Testament, goes on to command "all Christians of either sex not to presume to *think* (sentire), teach, or preach otherwise than according to what is contained in this Our Constitution." The same prohibition, couched in the very same words, occurs also in the Bull "Auctorem Fidei," issued (1794) by Pius VI. in condemnation of eighty-five propositions extracted from the decrees of the Synod of Pistoia. Lastly, to quote an instance from recent times, Pius IX. in the brief "Eximiam tuam," addressed by him (1857) to the Cardinal Archbishop of Cologne with reference to the proscription of Gunther's works by the Congregation of the Index, writes as follows:—

"This decree [of the Index], ratified by Our authority and promulgated by Our command, clearly ought to have sufficed to cause the whole question to be regarded as completely settled, and to have made all who glory in the name of Catholic understand that the doctrine contained in Gunther's books *could not be accounted as sound* (sinceram), and that no one thenceforth might lawfully defend and maintain this doctrine, or keep and read these books without the necessary faculties. And from this obligation of obedience and due submission no one could be regarded as exempt, either because in this same decree no propositions were branded by name, or because no definite and fixed censure was affixed to them. For the decree itself was sufficient ground that no one should think it open to him to depart in the slightest degree from what We have approved."

Hence, according to the teaching of the Sovereign Pontiff, the fact that a book has been proscribed by the Congregation of the Index with the Pope's approbation, and that the decree of condemnation has been promulgated by his command, ought to be proof enough to a Catholic of the unsoundness of the book. Surely the inference to be drawn from this is plain. If the Church teaches that a given book is unsound, we are bound interiorly as well as exteriorly to regard it as such.

The examples we have adduced are sufficient indications of the Church's mind and intention in her doctrinal condemnations. But it so happens that the whole question of her intention and our obligation was thoroughly sifted, and the truth placed in a still clearer light two centuries ago, on the occasion of the Jansenist heresy. We have already alluded to this controversy when speaking of the Church's infallibility in pronouncing upon dogmatic facts. The device by which the Jansenists sought to elude the censures of the Church and to escape formal exclusion from her communion, was, as we then remarked, by distinguishing between the *doctrine* of the five propositions and the *fact* of their being virtually contained in the Augustinus of Jansenius. They admitted the Church's right to pass sentence on the doctrine, and did not deny that they were bound to assent interiorly to her condemnation of it. But they maintained that it was beyond her power to determine the fact. And when she compelled them to subscribe a formulary, in which they professed to accept both the fact and the doctrine, they took refuge in the distinction of reserving their interior submission to the question of doctrine, and giving only the exterior obedience of a respectful silence to the question of fact, as though this latter point were a mere regulation of discipline. Their subterfuge, however, was formally condemned by Clement XI., in the Bull "Vineam Domini Sabaoth" (1715), as follows:—

"In order that for the future every occasion of error may be removed, and that all the children of the Catholic Church may learn to hear the Church, not by keeping silence only (for the impious also are silent in darkness), but by *interior obedience, which is the true obedience of an orthodox man,* We, by Apostolic authority, decree, declare, appoint, and ordain that this respectful silence by no means satisfies the obedience due to the pre-inserted Apostolic Constitutions [censuring the propositions of Jansenius], but that the sense of the book of Jansenius, condemned in the aforesaid propositions, and expressed in the words of these propositions, ought to be regarded as heretical, and condemned accordingly by all Christians, not in words only, but in their heart."

The Church's practical teaching, as the history of eighteen centuries exhibits it, affords us ample proof that she intends to oblige the faithful to interior assent, whenever she condemns a doctrine or a book on the ground of its deviation from the standard of the faith. And as she could not intend to bind us to interior submission, unless she knew with certainty that she could not err in her decree, the fact that she does require our assent is conclusive evidence that she is infallible in the censures she pronounces. But her infallibility and our consequent obligation of assent are brought home to us with still further evidence by the fact that all theologians agree in teaching that to deny her the power of infallibly censuring unsound doctrine is itself censurable. For we are bound to recognize in the moral unanimity of theologians, not merely the voice of a body of men deeply versed in theology, though even from this point of view alone it well deserves our veneration ; but, in a certain sense, the voice of the Ecclesia Docens, the Church as teacher, herself. This is what Pius IX. has laid down in the Brief "Tuas Libenter," addressed to the Archbishop of Munich (1863), on the occasion of the theological Congress held in that city, in which he declares that it is not enough for the learned in their writings "to venerate and receive those things which have been defined by express decrees of Œcumenical Councils and of the Roman Pontiffs," as well as "those things which are delivered as divinely revealed by the ordinary teaching (*magisterium*) of the Church dispersed throughout the world, and are therefore, by the universal and constant consent of Catholic theologians held to belong to the faith ;" but that they are likewise "bound in conscience to submit themselves both to the doctrinal decisions of the Pontifical Congregations, and also to those points of doctrine which, by the common and constant consent of Catholics, are held as theological truths and conclusions of such certainty that the opinions opposed to these points of doctrine, though they cannot be termed heretical, nevertheless deserve some other theological censure."

Now the Church's right and power infallibly to affix a theological note, whatever its specific nature may be, to unsound doctrine, is precisely one of these truths, the denial of which, according to the common judgment of theologians, is worthy of censure. About the note "heretical" there can be no question ; for if the Church is not infallible in declaring what is of faith, the whole edifice of the faith is shaken to its foundations. With regard to the lesser censures, the testimony of De Lugo, for it is not only as a witness to a fact that we quote him, is clear and distinct :—

"Theologians," he writes, "commonly allow that the Church's judgment in affixing these censures is certain. Bañes says that it is an error, or proximate to error, to say that the Church can err in this judgment; Malderus, that he who obstinately asserted it would be a heretic; Coninch, that this opinion of Malderus is very probable; Turrianus, that it is an error to affirm that the Pontiff can err in decreeing these censures. I also think it erroneous or proximate to error." (De Fide, Disp. 20, n. 108.)

Thus theologians with one consent agree that the opinion denying the Church's power to affix the minor censures infallibly is censurable; they only differ about the quality of the theological censure which it deserves. Hence, according to the principles laid down in the Brief of Pius IX. just quoted, we are bound to regard the Church as infallible in affixing the minor censures; and therefore, as a further consequence, to submit ourselves with interior assent to her decrees.

But besides all this, the words of Pius IX. in the Encyclical "Quanta cura" (1864) would be alone sufficient to place the question of the Church's intention beyond reasonable doubt. For the Pope, in his dogmatic letter to the bishops of Christendom, distinctly condemns "the audacity of those who contend that, without sin and without any sacrifice of the Catholic profession, *assent* and obedience may be refused to the judgments and decrees of the Apostolic See, whose object is declared to concern the Church's general good, and her rights and discipline." Now, obedience being a general term, may be interpreted as referring to a purely external submission. Assent, however, will admit of no such meaning. The only thing which it can mean is an internal conformity of the understanding to the object of the assent. It is this assent, or interior submission, which the Vicar of Christ declares cannot be refused to the Church's judgments and decrees without sin of so grave a character as to involve some sacrifice of the Christian profession. What more can an obedient child of the Church desire in evidence of the obligation which the Church intends to lay upon him by her doctrinal decrees and condemnations?

Since, as we have just seen, the Church requires us to yield assent to the decrees in which she judges and condemns unsound doctrines, we must next inquire what is the precise object to which she claims our assent. The answer to this is evident. We are bound to assent simply and solely to the particular point which the Church has ruled in her decree. If she declares an opinion heretical, we must believe it to be heretical; if erroneous, erroneous; if scandalous, scandalous; if temerarious, temerarious; and so forth. Again, if she simply condemns a doctrine or a book, without particularizing the note or censure which it deserves, we must interiorly regard it as unsound. Of course we may logically infer from the intrinsic nature of many of the censures by which she proscribes a doctrine, that the doctrine so proscribed is false; and may, therefore, as reasoning and reasonable men, be bound to regard it as such. Still its falsity is only an inference from her teaching, and not part of it. Hence it is not obligatory upon our belief in virtue of her decree.

The last thing which it remains for us to consider is whether the Church intends to oblige us to interior submission to her doctrinal judgments under pain of sin, and, if so, of what sin. No one who professes to be a Catholic can doubt that we are bound under grave sin to pay them at least an exterior submission. Even the Jansenists did not refuse to yield a "respectful silence" to decrees which they regarded as founded on error, and tyrannical. Nor, again, can it be disputed that a Catholic who declines to regard interiorly a doctrine as heretical, which the Church has condemned as such, is guilty of heresy. But is it sinful to refuse or to suspend assent to the Church's doctrinal pronouncements, which have for their object opinions not in formal and direct opposition to what is of faith? This is the only point on which it is possible to raise a question. And yet to state the case is to answer it. Almighty God has appointed the Church to be our teacher; He has guaranteed her teaching against error; and He has commanded us to obey her when she teaches. In the exercise of this her teaching office, she solemnly declares to us that a particular doctrine is faulty and censurable, and she distinctly orders us to believe that it deserves the censure which she has affixed to it. Placed in this position, with no alternative between obedience and disobedience, what is our duty? Surely, our Catholic instincts tell us that to disobey is to sin; and as to the quality of the sin we may learn its gravity from the words of Scripture: "It is like the sin of witchcraft to rebel, and like the crime of idolatry to refuse to obey" (1 Kings xv. 23). This is what Pius IX. has taught us in the Encyclical "Quanta cura," quoted above, in which he formally denies that "*assent* and obedience may be refused to the judgments and decrees of the Apostolic See, *without sin and without any sacrifice of the Catholic profession.*" If the Pope had only used the word "sin," we might have tried to fancy that he meant venial sin; but in adding the phrase, "any sacrifice of the Catholic profession," he has explained the nature of the sin to be a kind of apostasy, and thus shown us unmistakably that it must be mortal. We can say nothing stronger about the sinfulness of refusing an interior assent to the Church's judgment than what the Vicar of Christ has said.

VII.

We have now reached the term of these investigations. After contemplating the Church as our divinely-appointed teacher, intrusted with power to teach us infallibly all truth, and to guard us from error of every kind which may militate against the purity of the revealed deposit, we venerated in the Sovereign Pontiff, whether he speaks alone or with the approbation of an Œcumenical Council, the infallible organ and tribunal through which Christ ever guides His flock. Then we surveyed, first in general and afterwards in detail, the domain of her infallibility as teacher, and studied the ways in which she teaches, the nature of her doctrinal condemnations, and the obligation which her teaching imposes on us. And now all that remains is to offer, in conclusion, a few brief remarks on the practical bearings of the subject of which we have been treating. As a convenient mode of doing this, we will choose the form of answers to objections which may possibly have suggested themselves against the doctrine which we have been endeavouring to set forth.

1. First, then, it may be said, that to oblige Catholics under pain of mortal sin to submit their intellect to the Church's teaching on a variety of matters philosophical, political, scientific, and the like, which are only remotely connected with faith and morals, is to lay upon them an intolerable burden, such as will crush out all activity of mind and be a perpetual hamper to them in all scientific researches.—To this objection it may be answered that it really begs the question; for all its force comes from the implied assumption that the Church is not infallible in such matters. If she is infallible, as she claims by her acts to be, what she teaches concerning these things is absolute truth. And no addition to our stock of truth, whencesoever it comes, and on whatever grounds it rests, can justly be regarded as an intellectual burden. On the contrary, it is an intellectual benefit, as tending to clear our views, to save us from possible errors, and to advance us in the pursuit of truth. The difficulty is at bottom precisely the same as that which non-Catholics feel about the Church's teaching in matters of faith. To them it seems a tyranny in her to oblige reasonable beings to believe dogmas which do not rest for their evidence on natural reason. And it would be a tyranny, if we granted their assumption that the Church is fallible in matters of faith. The Jansenists, too, made the very same objection in their day, as appears from the ninety-fourth pro-

position of the Jansenist Quesnel, condemned and censured by Clement XI., in the Bull " Unigenitus." " Nothing," writes Quesnel, "gives a worse opinion of the Church to her enemies than to see in her the belief of the faithful domineered over, and divisions fostered, on account of things which neither injure faith nor morals." He alludes to the decrees of the Apostolic See, obliging the faithful to accept with inward assent the dogmatic fact, that the five condemned propositions of Jansenius, extracted from the "Augustinus," really represented the sense of the author as it was to be gathered from his book. The conduct of the Church towards the Jansenists was only not tyrannical, because she was infallible in decreeing what she required them to believe. The objection, then, which we have been considering is manifestly groundless, except indeed on the baseless hypothesis that the Church's infallibility does not extend to matters which have only a remote connection with the faith,—a point which we have already treated at sufficient length.

2. But the view put forward in these pages is novel, for until quite recently no one ever heard of the Church claiming to teach anything infallibly except dogmas of faith and general principles of moralty.—In reply, we admit that to a certain extent it is novel in England, and for a very evident reason. Our controversy in this country has hitherto lain almost entirely with Protestants, about the elementary dogmas of the faith. We have not had our attention called to other subjects. But a doctrine which is taught by the Church herself, as the acts of the Sovereign Pontiff and the Catholic Episcopate abundantly

show, cannot be termed absolutely new. In fact, our whole line of argument has gone to disprove this accusation of novelty. For we have not rested our case on mere theory or the dicta of theological writers, but on the actual teaching and practice of the Church.

3. *But it will backen Protestant inquirers, if they should hear that the Church claims to possess infallibility over such a wide range of subjects.*—We answer: Is the doctrine true or is it false? If true, to hide it from inquirers would be to deceive them. They have a right to know what claims the Church has upon their obedience. And if it backen some who would fain obtain admission to the fold with the least possible sacrifice of their private judgment, it will attract others, who, weary of their fruitless searchings after a truth which is perpetually slipping from their grasp, yearn for nothing so much as an infallible teacher, whose eye will be ever on them, and whose warning voice will never fail them, let them wander as they may through the whole field of human thought and speculation.

4. *But the subject is so abstruse that none but a professed theologian has a right to an opinion upon it.*—No doubt it has its difficulties, as all theological subjects have. But it has its practical side also, which is within every one's comprehension. How many deep and difficult questions the dogma of the Incarnation involves! and yet all well-instructed Catholics have a clear and definite view of this mystery, and one, moreover, very fertile in practical consequences. So, in like manner, the doctrine of the Church's authority as teacher, which is immeasurably less abstruse than the dogma of the Incarnation, can be ex-

plained to any one quite easily, so far as its general principles and practical bearings are concerned.

5. *But how much more prudent it would have been to let the question alone, instead of thus forcing it upon public notice.*—Questions sometimes cannot be let alone External circumstances compel us to entertain them, and they give us no peace until we have answered them. The question before us is one of these. Let us look at the facts of the case. The Church in fulfilment of what she regards as her bounden duty and right, has never ceased, especially of late years, to lift up her voice again and again to condemn the multitudinous errors which are everywhere silently sapping the foundations of social and political life and uprooting the first principles of natural ethics and religion. It is to us, her children, that her warnings are principally addressed. How then is it possible for us to remain deaf and insensible to her voice? Nay, even if we had been inclined to shut our ears, which God forbid, the very storm of indignation and howls of rage and abuse with which each fresh condemnation of error has been greeted by its upholders would have forced us to attention. But when once we have realized the fact of these pronouncements, how can we escape the question, —What obligation, in conscience, do they lay upon us? If we would we could not ignore it. Perhaps we will not put the question to ourselves; but how can we hinder it from being put to us, sooner or later, by our non-Catholic friends? And it is a fair question for them to ask, considering the relation in which they know we stand to the Church as Catholics. But when put, the question must be answered. To suspend our assent to what the

Church has ruled, unless for a short time in order to inquire into our duty, is to deny her claim as infallible teacher—it is to take our side and answer the question practically. If, then, the question cannot be let alone and hushed up, no blame can deservedly attach to those who try to explain what is the Church's doctrine, and so clear up the path of duty.

6. But at any rate the question is an open one, and therefore the golden rule comes into play, "in necessary things let there be unity, but in doubtful things liberty."— Far from this our whole argument has gone to show that the Church herself does not regard it as an open question, but that she requires of her children, under pain of mortal sin, an absolute and interior submission to what she rules on points of doctrine, which are only remotely and indirectly connected with the revealed deposit. No doubt Catholics who deny her infallibility in such matters will treat her words not only with exterior, but a certain amount of interior respect. They will neither rudely set aside nor contemn her teaching. For who would treat an earthly parent thus, how much less the Spouse of Christ and their spiritual mother? But granting this to the utmost, they will refuse, and on the supposition of her fallibility they will be consistent in refusing an absolute interior assent to her decrees. The duty they owe to truth will prevent them from an unreasoning submission, and they will be bound to keep their judgment free, however much they may incline it towards the Church's side in deference to her authority. But this is not the kind of submission which will satisfy the Church. She insists upon an interior assent to her judgments and

decrees, and condemns those who say that this may be withheld "without sin and without any sacrifice of the Catholic profession." How, then, can this be an open question among Catholics?

7. But at least the question is unimportant and unpractical.—We reply that, looked at as it affects our relation to the Church herself, it cannot be an unimportant thing to have the conclusion forced upon us that she practically claims to speak infallibly on a variety of subjects, about which we believe that she is not infallible, and that she is in the habit of demanding our interior assent to her teaching without any guarantee that what she teaches is the truth. To discover, as we imagine, that she is imposing upon us in any point must create a general feeling of mistrust towards her. And mistrust of her is a dangerous feeling, considering that her authority enters as a condition into every act of faith we make. By degrees, too, a feeling of soreness towards her might easily grow up in us, as if she were dealing with us hardly, in thus obliging us to outward conformity with her judgments, and refusing to recognize our fancied right of inward dissent; and all this because she will insist on claiming infallibility in matters where she had no just title to it. Then, perhaps, out of our very reverence for her, and our desire to find an excuse for conduct which seems to us so unworthy of her, we might go on to draw a distinction between her authority in the abstract, and the persons actually vested with this authority; and while exculpating her, we might ascribe what grated on us to their imprudence or infirmity. The result of all this would be an undutiful and unfilial spirit towards the Church, very

different from the self-forgetting, childlike loyalty which ought to animate us.

But besides the way in which this question affects our relations to the Church, it has other practical bearings which are far from unimportant. Thus if we believe that God has given us in the Church a teacher who has the power to condemn, without the possibility of mistake, erroneous doctrine in all subjects connected even remotely with faith and morals, our whole position towards philosophy and science will be practically different from what it would be if we held that God had given us no such teacher. On the latter hypothesis we should study, speculate, and work out our results in a free and independent spirit, trusting to reason alone to correct the mistakes of reason, and ready to accept as true any conclusions we might arrive at, so long as they were not in direct opposition to some distinctly defined dogma of the faith. On the other hand, if we recognize an infallible teacher in the Church, we shall be careful to pursue our investigations in a spirit of docile submission to the guidance she may afford us, and, preferring her light to our own, we shall at once reject as untenable any opinion, however dear to us, on which she has set her mark of condemnation.

Again, our views on the subject of education will be very considerably influenced by the opinions which we may hold on the subject of the Church's infallibility as teacher. Of course as Catholics we should in any case prefer that education was carried on under the Church's supervision and control. Still we shall be far less jealous of a system of mixed education and less fearful of non-Catholic influence and teaching being brought to bear on our youth in colleges and universities, if we hold that secular science forms a world of its own, external to the domain of faith, and not subject even indirectly to the Church's infallible teaching office.

Again, in regard to social and political questions, if we believe that the Church may err in what she teaches concerning them, her judgments will not weigh much with us, and we shall never think of giving up any of our opinions because they are in contradiction to her decisions. On the other hand, if we look upon her teaching on these matters as necessarily true, we shall, undoubtedly, take pains to ascertain what she has taught and what she has condemned, and shape our views and conduct accordingly. And this is no imaginary case. In every country doctrines fundamentally at variance with the principles of the faith are daily taking deeper hold of the popular mind, and gaining ground among men of thought and action equally. The whole atmosphere is, in fact, impregnated with them. Catholics, as well as others, are subject to these baneful influences, and the temptation comes to many, especially to those whose life is spent among non-Catholics, to try to combine these doctrines with the faith, and thus to go along with the spirit of the age without renouncing their Catholic profession. The Vicar of Christ has indeed never failed to warn the faithful on repeated occasions of the danger to which they are thus exposed, and he has formally condemned as erroneous, the assertion that "the Roman Pontiff can and ought to reconcile himself and come to terms with progress, liberalism, and modern civilization" (Syllabus, Prop. lxxx.). Now whether Catholics yield or not to this temptation will depend very much on the view they take of the Church's infallibility in questions of politics, education, and science. The warnings of the Pope will fall on heedless or obedient ears according as the hearers deny or believe that the Church has received from God the power and right to pronounce infallibly upon matters which bear only indirectly upon the faith. But if this be so, it follows that the question which has been occupying us is of incalculable importance and of the highest practical interest. It may be inconvenient to consider it, but it well deserves consideration.

And now our task is ended. May the Spirit of truth pardon its shortcomings, and graciously accept this humble endeavour to set forth in words the greatness and fulness of the gift which He has given us in the Church our teacher. May He, who "as an unction" from above "abides" in the members of the Church and "teaches us concerning all things" (1 John ii. 27), so guide the minds and hearts of all in whom He dwells, that we, being "of the same mind, having the same charity, of one accord, thinking the selfsame thing" (Phil. ii. 2), may ever "keep the unity of the Spirit in the bond of peace," "with all humility and meekness, bearing with one another in charity" (Eph. iv. 2).

THE END.

WYMAN AND SONS, PRINTERS, GREAT QUEEN STREET, LONDON, W.C.

www.ingramcontent.com/pod-product-compliance
Lightning Source LLC
Chambersburg PA
CBHW021937160426
43195CB00011B/1120